August 4th, 2007

Thank you for attending my graduation celebration! One of the lessons I learnt in college is how privileged we are; I hope that through this book, you too will appreciate it. Enjoy this anthology by fortunate Indians for the not-so-fortunate.

Respectfully,
Bharati Kalasapudi

A POEM FOR CRY

A POEM FOR CRY

FAVOURITE POEMS
OF
FAMOUS INDIANS

Foreword by

Amartya Sen

Compiled and Edited by

Avanti Maluste and Sudeep Doshi

CHILD RIGHTS AND YOU

PENGUIN
VIKING

VIKING
Published by the Penguin Group
Penguin Books India Pvt. Ltd, 11 Community Centre, Panchsheel Park, New Delhi110 017, India
Penguin Group (USA) Inc., 375 Hudson Street, New York, New York 10014, USA
Penguin Group (Canada), 90 Eglinton Avenue East, Suite 700, Toronto, Ontario, M4P 2Y3, Canada (a division of Pearson Penguin Canada Inc.)
Penguin Books Ltd, 80 Strand, London WC2R 0RL, England
Penguin Ireland, 25 St Stephen's Green, Dublin 2, Ireland (a division of Penguin Books Ltd)
Penguin Group (Australia), 250 Camberwell Road, Camberwell, Victoria 3124, Australia (a division of Pearson Australia Group Pty Ltd)
Penguin Group (NZ), cnr Airborne and Rosedale Roads, Albany, Auckland 1310, New Zealand (a division of Pearson New Zealand Ltd)
Penguin Group (South Africa) (Pty) Ltd, 24 Sturdee Avenue, Rosebank, Johannesburg 2196, South Africa

Penguin Books Ltd, Registered Offices: 80 Strand, London WC2R 0RL, England

First published in Viking by Penguin Books India 2006

Page 213 is an extension of the copyright page.

10 9 8 7 6 5 4 3 2

ISBN-13: 978-0-67004-998-1 ISBN-10: 0-67004-998-0

For sale in the Indian Subcontinent and Singapore only

Design by Yellow Ink Design, Mumbai
Typeset by S.R. Enterprises, New Delhi
Printed at Gopson Papers Ltd

Every child comes with the message that god is not yet discouraged of man.

Rabindranath Tagore

CONTENTS

ACKNOWLEDGEMENTS xiv
FOREWORD xvi
PREFACE xxi

1. WE ARE SEVEN 1
WILLIAM WORDSWORTH
2. THE CITY 5
C.P. CAVAFY
3. THE RUBAIYAT 7
OMAR KHAYYAM
4. *FROM* THE LAY OF THE LAST MINSTREL 16
SIR WALTER SCOTT
5. THE CHILD ANGEL 17
RABINDRANATH TAGORE
6. THE POEM 18
RABINDRANATH TAGORE
7. DAFFODILS 19
WILLIAM WORDSWORTH
8. WHERE THE MIND IS WITHOUT FEAR 21
RABINDRANATH TAGORE
9. MERI AAWAAZ SUNO 24
KAIFI AZMI
10. KYA BHOOLOON KYA YAAD KAROON? 27
HARIVANSH RAI BACHCHAN
11. IF 32
RUDYARD KIPLING
12. THE ROAD NOT TAKEN 35
ROBERT FROST
13. HIMALAYA KE PRATI 37
RAMDHARI SINGH 'DINKAR'
14. EPITAPH ON A TYRANT 46
W. H AUDEN
15. LEAD KINDLY LIGHT 47
CARDINAL NEWMAN
16. SHINE LIKE A STAR 48
17. FAERY SONG 49
JOHN KEATS
18. INTEZAAR 50
SAAHIR LUDHIANVI
19. PATTERNS 52
AMY LOWELL
20. A FAREWELL 56
ANONYMOUS

21. CHILDREN'S EYES 57
TOM KRAUSE

22. MITHYATVA 58
NARSINH MEHTA

23. THE HOUND OF HEAVEN 61
FRANCIS THOMPSON

24. *FROM* DIES SLOWLY 67
PABLO NERUDA

25. THE LOVE SONG OF J. ALFRED PRUFROCK 68
T.S. ELIOT

26. WALK ALONE 74
RABINDRANATH TAGORE

27. THE CAPTAIN 75
NADIR GODREJ

28. COSMIC MURMUR 77
SHIELA GUJRAL

29. BOOKS 79
GULZAR

30. A STRANGE PROBLEM 82
KANWAR NARAIN

31. JANA GANA MANA 84
RABINDRANATH TAGORE

32. FOOTPRINTS IN THE SAND 85
MARY STEVENSON

33. *FROM* BURNT NORTON 87
T.S. ELIOT

34. THE NATIONAL PRAYER 89
A.P.J. ABDUL KALAM

35. OZYMANDIAS 91
PERCY BYSSHE SHELLEY

36. ABRAHAM LINCOLN'S LETTER TO HIS SON'S TEACHER 92
ABRAHAM LINCOLN

37. KARMAYOGA 95
FROM THE BHAGAVAD GITA

38. GUIDE TO THE BODHISATTAVA'S WAY OF LIFE 96
MASTER SHANTIDEVA

39. SONNET 16 97
WILLIAM SHAKESPEARE

40. MORNING EXPRESS 98
SIEGFRIED SASSOON

41. MEN OF GENIUS 100

42. AISE HAIN SUKH SAPAN HAMARE 102
PANDIT NARENDRA SHARMA

43. SAY NOT THE STRUGGLE NAUGHT AVAILETH 104
ARTHUR HUGH CLOUGH

44. KRANTICHA–JAYJAYKAR 106
KUSUMAGRAJ

45. EDUCATION 112
TIRUVALLUVAR

46. CELEBRATING 113
SRI SRI RAVI SHANKAR

47. THE WORLD'S NEED 114
ELLA WHEELER WILCOX

48. SONNET FOR JEHANGIR 115
DOM MORAES

49. UNDER ONE SMALL STAR 116
WISLAWA SZYMBORSKA

50. AND STILL I RISE 118
MAYA ANGELOU

51. THE SOLDIER 120
RUPERT BROOKE

52. THE SECOND COMING 121
W.B. YEATS

53. AAJ AGAR KHAMOSH RAHE TO . . . 123
SAAHIR LUDHIANVI

54. THE EXEQUY 125
HENRY KING

55. THE PIED PIPER OF HAMELIN 129
ROBERT BROWNING

56. ANTARA MOMO BIKOSHITO KORO 140
RABINDRANATH TAGORE

57. CLOSING THE GAP 142

58. THE BALLAD OF FATHER GILLIGAN 143
W.B. YEATS

59. HAR GUMA HAI AETBAAR 146
JAGJIT SINGH

60. WHO 148
SRI AUROBINDO

61. O NISSANG MAMETAR 151
AGYEYA

62. SPEAK GENTLY 164
DAVID BATES

63. MAN'S TESTAMENT 167
ADAM LINDSAY GORDON

64. *FROM* GEETANJALI 168
RABINDRANATH TAGORE

65. ODE TO A NIGHTINGALE 170
JOHN KEATS

66. REEDS OF INNOCENCE 173
WILLIAM BLAKE

67. Sachin 174
Ramesh Tendulkar

68. Dulce Et Decorum Est 175
Wilfred Owen

69. Hari Bhari Doob Par 177
Atal Bihari Vajpayee

70. Ulysses 180
Alfred Tennyson

71. All You Who Sleep Tonight 184
Vikram Seth

72. The Peddler's Caravan 185
William Brighty Rands

73. Stopping by Woods on a Snowy Evening 186
Robert Frost

74. Youth 187
Samuel Ullman

75. Merrow Down 189
Rudyard Kipling

76. Maru Satakam 191
Amaru

77. Ye Bachcha Kaisa Bachcha Hai 192
Ibne Insha

78. Banalata Sen 196
Jibanananda Das

79. My Heart Leaps up 198
William Wordsworth

80. Gayatri Mantra 199

81. Elegy Written in a Country Courtyard 200
Thomas Gray

82. Quote 206
Ella Wheeler Wilcox

83. The Treasured Writings of Khalil Gibran: The Playground of Life 207
Khalil Gibran

84. The Heart of the Tree 209
Henry Ceyler Bunner

85. Brahma 211
Ralph Waldo Emerson

86. On the Banks of the Indrayani 212
G.D. Madgulkar

Copyright Acknowledgements 213

Contributors

L.K. Advani 45
Mani Shankar Aiyar 6
M.J. Akbar 15
P.C. Alexander 16
Tina Ambani 17
Baba Amte 18
Mulk Raj Anand 20
Vishwanathan Anand 20
Tariq Ansari 21
Shabana Azmi 26
Amitabh Bachchan 31
Lord Bagri 33
Rahul Bajaj 21
Manvinder Singh Banga 36
Kiran Bedi 4
Shyam Benegal 46
Ela R. Bhatt 47
Subhash Chandra 48
Justice Y.V. Chandrachud 49
Yash Chopra 51
Nana Chudasama 22
Farzana Contractor 33
Charles Correa 55
Gerson da Cunha 56
His Holiness the Dalai Lama 96
Tarla Dalal 57
Tarun Das 66
Shobhaa Dé 67
Lord Meghnad Desai 73
Rahul Dravid 33
Sonia Gandhi 74
Adi Godrej 33
Nadir Godrej 76
Parmeshwar Godrej 34
Harsh Goenka 36
I.K. Gujral 78
Gulzar 81
Shekhar Gupta 83
Anna Hazare 84
Indira Hinduja 86
Karan Johar 20
Pandit Bhimsen Joshi 212
Prahlad Kakkar 88
A.P.J. Abdul Kalam 90
K.V. Kamath 91

Aamir Khan 22
Shah Rukh Khan 94
Faqir Kohli 95
Uday Kotak 36
Anand Mahindra 101
Lata Mangeshkar 103
Justice Sujata Manohar 104
Sonal Mansingh 60
R.A. Mashelkar 184
Zubin Mehta 185
Anjolie Ela Menon 73
Mario Miranda 186
Sunil Bharti Mittal 188
Dom Moraes 190
Madhavi Mudgal 191
Shubha Mudgal 195
Pritish Nandy 197
Jayant Narlikar 198
Nandan Nilekani 199
Derek O' Brien 205
Alyque Padamsee 73
K.C. Pant 186
Piyush Pandey 206
Deepak Parekh 208
I.G. Patel 210
Justice R.S. Pathak 211
Medha Patkar 111
Anand Patwardhan 22
Azim Premji 36
Cho Ramaswami 112
Julio Ribeiro 114
Aruna Roy 22
Prannoy Roy 22
Jehangir M. Sabavala 115
Leela Samson 117
Malavika Sangghvi 119
Mallika Sarabhai 23
Rajdeep Sardesai 120
Jyotiraditya M. Scindia 86
Amartya Sen 97, 99
Aparna Sen 121
Teesta Setalvad 124
Vikram Seth 128
Naseeruddin Shah 139
Viren J. Shah 23
Pandit Ravi Shankar 141
Sri Sri Ravi Shankar 113

Kiran Mazumdar Shaw	23
Laxman Shreshtha	142
Pesi Shroff	145
Jagjit Singh	147
Karan Singh	150
Khushwant Singh	205
L.M. Singhvi	163
Brinda Somaya	165
Soli. J. Sorabjee	167
Kavita Krishnamurthy Subramaniam	23
Sharmila Tagore	169
Tarun Tahiliani	172
Raveena Tandon	173
Sachin Tendulkar	174
Shashi Tharoor	176
Atal Bihari Vajpayee	179
Fareed Zakaria	183

Acknowledgements

It is truly wonderful to watch a project develop from a nascent possibility to a tangible reality. The fact that *A Poem For CRY* can be called the latter, is testament to the hard work and support of several people who deserve our gratitude. Without them, this book would have remained a distant dream.

A debt of gratitude to Ingrid Srinath, Yogita Verma and Admiral Johnson at CRY for recognizing the promise of this book and taking it on with professionalism, superb dedication and optimism.

To Penguin India for their endorsement of this unique venture and constant backing.

To Namrata Bhawnani for editing, T.N. Ganapathy for data entry and Roweena Bhatia-Yellow Ink for layout and design.

To all the contributors, for taking time out of their busy schedules to reflect, awaken the artists within and send us profound and insightful responses, as well as a lot of uplifting support for our cause.

To Suresh Parikh and Mihir Doshi who gave invaluable guidance and formed the backbone of this book.

To Sudha and Jagdish Doshi, Lalita, Kanan and Sanjay Parikh, Bala and Priyamvada Doshi, Amishi Doshi and Kshama Ajmera, for their steadfast confidence in the success of this book, their inexhaustible and inspirational sanguinity, and for all the small suggestions that made a big difference.

To Rajni Bala, O. P. Jain, Haadi Kizilbaash, Devu Kothari, Rajni Bakshi, Lina Ashar and Abhik and Shukla Mitra, for their persistence in helping us to contact several contributors and for their ongoing enthusiasm for the book. To Abin K. Das, G.N. Pande and Yash Kohli for help in translations.

To Pushpa Balan, Virna Rodrigues, Salma Abbas, Magan Patel, Harshad Shah, Suresh Lokhande, Ramchandra and Anil for all the typing, paper work, follow-up phone calls, address searches and transport.

Thanks also to Shilpa Hirani, Panna Jhaveri, I.M. Kadri, Jyoti Khanna, Amy Madon, Niyati Mehta, Bimal Parekh, Sevanti Parekh, Alok Rakhiyan and Narayan Varma for their assistance and effort.

And to our parents, Mridula and Nandan Maluste and Sucheta and Viral Doshi, who believed wholeheartedly in this book from the beginning and gave us the conviction to drive it forward and reach out to the children of CRY. They are as responsible for the existence of this book as we are.

Foreword

'All a poet can do today is warn,' wrote Wilfred Owen, who captured so very well the sadness of human lives amidst violence and war. The tragedy of violence is made even more unbearable by its glorification, which is used so effectively by the architects of violence, particularly in recruiting foot-soldiers for savagery. Since we encounter exaltation of brutality more or less continuously in the turbulent world in which we—and our children—live, it is good to see among the poems selected for this anthology for CRY, Owen's bitter but visionary poem, 'Dulce et Decorum est' (selected by Shashi Tharoor).

My friend, you will not tell with such high zest
To children ardent for some desperate glory,
The old lie: Dulce et Decorum est
Pro Patria Mori.

Horace's rousing endorsement of the honour of death for (or allegedly for) one's country translates easily into similar celebrations of the imagined honour of dying—and killing others—for one's religion or community and other mesmerizing causes. The evocative appeal of such sentiment is devastatingly used today, as in the past, to entrap the young in a modernized magnification of the nasty ways of the old. Owen's warning has as much contemporary relevance right now as it had when he himself was facing the horrors of the First World War which would ultimately take his own life.

This is a wonderful collection of poems, and I must take the opportunity to express my appreciation of the imaginative initiative taken by Avanti Maluste and Sudeep Doshi—and their collaborators—in producing this collection, through involving people in active selection. The poems are of interest not only for the merits of the poems themselves, but also for telling us something about the commitments and priorities of the selectors that are reflected in their choices. We live not only by our own thoughts formulated in isolation, but also by the ideas and phrases of others that resonate and move us.

Wilfred Owen's mother, Susan, wrote to Rabindranath Tagore in 1920, describing her son's final departure for the war that would eventually cost him his life. Through the nastiness of the desolation of war, young Wilfred could still see the beauty of nature and civilization. He went to war 'looking towards the sun-glorified sea - looking towards France'. Susan Owen told Rabindranath that Wilfred said good-bye with 'those wonderful words of yours-beginning at "When I go from hence, let this be my parting word".' When the pocket book of her dead son, recovered in the battlefield, was sent to Susan Owen, she found (she wrote to Tagore) 'these words written in his dear writing - with your name beneath'.

If one can find the right poems, quoting someone else can be as much an expression of one's deeper self as anything one can write oneself. This is a remarkable collection not only for the beauty and reach of the poems themselves, but also for what it tells us about many people who have been active in one walk of life or another, since the selections allow us to have a quick peek into their minds. When, to take one example, Shyam Benegal quotes W.H. Auden's description of sycophancy and blindness that underpin tyranny ('When he laughed, respectable senators burst with laughter,/ And when he cried the little children died in the streets'), he tells us not only about the political dejection of the once rhapsodic Auden, nor only about the violence and repression in which the world has been caught for so long, he gives us also a glimpse of the dedication that can move a creative artist like Benegal to portray predicaments and defiance with such skill and vision.

The poems selected have other interests as well, and some can arouse rather extensive reflection. Consider, for example, Pandit Ravi

Shankar's choice of a Bengali poem—uncompromisingly presented without translation—by Rabindranath Tagore, summoning 'inner development' that makes us awake ('jagroto'), uplifted ('uddoto') and fearless ('nirbhoy'). This, in fact, has an aesthetic reach that is worth noting, since Tagore's innovative use of the Bengali language is a subject in which even those who cannot read Bengali can have general intellectual interest. Anyone familiar with the spectacular battle scenes in the Mahabharata (in Sanskrit or in translation) would, of course, know how often various weapons—arrows, spears, maces—are 'uplifted' ('udyata' in Sanskrit, reduced to 'uddoto' in Bengali) in readiness for use. But Rabindranath's transfer of that epithet to describe the need for human beings to uplift themselves—and to be ready—had not been, I believe, common in Bengali earlier. It is, to be sure, common enough now, and Ravi Shankar's selection gives us the occasion to remember how often Tagore not only presented new ideas, but also helped develop the language for their expression. That Shakespeare did this often enough in English is well recognised, but there is some scope for a fuller understanding of how Rabindranath did this too. It may also help to explain a little the aesthetic as well as intellectual loyalties that Tagore evokes in Bangladesh and east India (something that readers elsewhere often find so mystifying).

The power of Rabindranath's ideas is indeed well celebrated outside as well as inside his Bengali habitat, but in terms of language and literature, the reception of Rabindranath in the English media has been persistently problematic, largely because of the fact that subtleties of language are so hard to preserve in translating poetry. It is, therefore, nice to find what can be seen as a balancing act in Ravi Shankar's choice of a Bengali poem without the compromise of translation: there is also some delicious irony in finding such a marvellous example of graceful parochialism by the most universalist of our great musicians.

Tagore's poems, quoted in English, do of course frequent these pages, because of the force and relevance of his ideas. I was happy and also amused to see that one of my favourite poems of all time (Tagore's invocation of freedom and openness 'Where the Mind Is Without Fear') was selected by no less than a dozen contributors: Tariq Ansari, Rahul Bajaj, Nana Chudasma, Aamir Khan, Anand Patwardhan, Aruna Roy, Prannoy Roy, Mallika Sarabhai, Viren Shah, Kiran Mazumdar Shaw, Kavita Krishnamurthy Subramaniam, and Sharmila Tagore. When I quoted the same poem in the remarks I had to make at the Nobel Banquet in Stockholm in 1998, I was aware that Subramanyan Chandrasekhar, the magnificent astrophysicist, had quoted it already in his own Nobel Banquet speech in 1983. Bowing to his precedence (not to mention his overwhelming intellectual superiority), I ended up, in fact, quoting Chandrasekhar's quoting of Tagore.

The poems have evocative appeals of other kinds as well. Since I have read Kaifi Azmi only in translation, it is nice to have the opportunity of reading one of his poems in Devnagari script, selected by his daughter Shabana. But equally importantly, the occasion of the poem, the funeral procession of Jawaharlal Nehru, reminds us of a piercing moment in Indian history. Personally, it took me back to that day in the summer of 1964 in Bangkok, where I was then giving some lectures, when an Egyptian doctor who was in the same hotel came and gave me the news, in a voice drowned in misery. It took me back to that political world of the beginning of an alliance of the poor and the non-aligned in the world, in which India was acting together with Egypt and Ghana (an implausible combination, except in this one respect), where Nehru's leadership was widely celebrated.

It is fashionable now to see Nehru as the author of many blunders that have occurred in India. Even if there are some elements of plausibility in those admonishments, it is quite absurd not to see the power of Nehru's large vision for India, combined with his global commitment, which informed Nehru's understanding of the future of India (something that had moved my Egyptian acquaintance so much). Not least of that commitment was to try to bring modern science and technology to the young of poor countries like India, of which the early Indian Institutes of Technology, which were very much the results of Nehru's initiative, were a part. To celebrate India's current success in globalized technology without looking into the imaginative developments that have made this success possible is to miss out a critically important link. Kaifi Azmi's message about children holding 'the future in their hands' is a huge vision, of which some parts are easily seen (like internet cafes right across the country), while other parts have remained obscure and neglected, in great need of a fuller understanding and cultivation (like transforming our 'country of first boys' into a nation where every child receives a decent education).

I must not go on, evocative as this collection of poems is. It is a privilege for me to be associated with this wonderful joint effort on behalf of a great organization which does so much to help precarious and vulnerable children. So I end by expressing my appreciation of the two editors and, of course, of CRY itself, but also by thanking all those who have participated in this engaging collaborative effort to put poems together. As the beautiful poem of Pablo Neruda (chosen by Shobhaa De) says, 'being alive requests a much bigger effort than the simple fact of breathing.' That effort, for ourselves and for others, not only needs support, but also some enthusiastic celebration.

Harvard University **Amartya Sen**

Preface

The motivating antecedent for this book was *Lifelines*, a bestseller during the 1980s. *Lifelines* was the brainchild of a group of students from Wesley College in Dublin who, over several years, collected poems from global celebrities for the benefit of charities around the world.

CRY—Child Rights and You—has for over twenty-five years championed the cause of underprivileged children in India. We grew up supporting this cause, and wanted to make a positive difference that could not merely be written off as a paycheck. With the success of *Lifelines* to guide us, a similar venture evolved, involving prominent Indians and the objective of donating the royalties from the sale of the book to CRY.

CRY, especially then chief executive Pervin Varma and her successor Ingrid Srinath, were enthusiastic about making the book a reality. After Penguin India graciously agreed to play publisher, we had a firm foundation for the project. Next, came the sometimes daunting task of tracking down and requesting India's prominent citizens for their poems.

We began at the very apex, with the president of India, Dr A. P. J. Abdul Kalam, who promptly responded with one of his own poems. This was just the impetus we needed: spurred, we wrote, e-mailed, phoned, even met more than three hundred Indians around the globe with the help and support of CRY, our families and friends.

The project gained momentum over the next two years, and persistence saw the manuscript materialize. The eclectic collection of poetry reflects the sweep and diversity of contributors: politicians, authors, sportsmen, entrepreneurs, industrialists, musicians and artists. Each donated a touching, often profound response dedicated to a common cause. Unfortunately, some notable names are missing from this roster, some because they were inaccessible, and others simply said that they did not have a favourite poem. To those who did contribute, however, we are sincerely grateful. Perhaps most notably, we would like to thank Amartya Sen, who, while traversing continents fielded an endless stream of e-mails and found the time to pen the moving foreword that captured the heart of this project and even (we dare say) validated it.

This anthology that you hold is the result of the hard work of dozens of people. Ultimately, we hope it conveys the richness of the art of poetry and a fleeting glimpse into the minds of some of the people that make India proud, because, as W. H. Auden said in *In Memory of W.B. Yeats* (1940):

'For poetry makes nothing happen: it survives
In the valley of its making where executives
Would never want to tamper, flows on south
From ranches of isolation and the busy griefs,
Raw towns that we believe and die in; it survives,
A way of happening, a mouth.'

By buying this book, for your bookshelf or as a gift, you support CRY and the future of India's children. We are privileged to put it into your hands, and hope you enjoy reading this collection as much as we enjoyed compiling it.

Mumbai
August 2006

Avanti Maluste
and
Sudeep Doshi

We Are Seven 1

A simple child,
That lightly draws its breath,
And feels its life in every limb,
What should it know of death?

I met a little cottage Girl:
She was eight years old, she said;
Her hair was thick with many a curl
That clustered round her head.

She had a rustic, woodland air,
And she was wildly clad:
Her eyes were fair, and very fair;
–Her beauty made me glad.

'Sisters and brothers, little Maid
How many may you be?'
'How many? Seven in all,' she said,
And wondering looked at me.

'And where are they? I pray you tell.'
She answered, 'Seven are we;
And two of us at Conway dwell,
And two are gone to sea'.

'Two of us in the church-yard lie,
My sister and my brother;
And, in the church-yard cottage, I
Dwell near them with my mother'.

'You say that two at Conway dwell,
And two are gone to sea,
Yet ye are seven! - I pray you tell,
Sweet Maid, how this may be.'

Then did the little Maid reply,
'Seven girls and boys are we;
Two of us in the church-yard lie,
Beneath the church-yard tree.'

'You run above, my little Maid,
Your limbs they are alive;
If two are in the church-yard laid,
Then ye are only five.'

'Their graves are green, they may be seen,'
The little maid replied,
Twelve steps from my mother's door
And they are side by side.

'My stockings there I often knit,
My kerchief there I hem;
And there upon the ground I sit,
And sing a song to them.

'And often after sun-set, Sir,
When it is light and fair,
I take my little porringer,
And eat my supper there.'

'The first that died was sister Jane;
In bed she moaning lay,
Till God released her of her pain;
And then she went away.

'So in the church-yard she was laid;
And, when the grass was dry,
Together round her grave we played,
My brother John and I

'And when the ground was white with snow,
And I could run and slide,
My brother John was forced to go,
And he lies by her side.'

'How many are you, then,' said I,
'If they two are in heaven?'
Quick was the little Maid's reply,
'Oh Master! We are seven.'

'But they are dead; those two are dead!
Their spirits are in heaven!'
'Twas throwing words away; for still
The little Maid would have her will,
And say, 'Nay, we are seven!'

William Wordsworth

Contributed By:

Kiran Bedi - broke new ground by being the first Indian woman to join the Indian Police Service in 1972. In 1993, as inspector general of Asia's biggest penitentiary, the Tihar jail, she sought to humanize its otherwise despicable conditions. She introduced programmes for the inmates on basic education, meditation, yoga and drama. For her efforts, Kiran Bedi won the Ramon Magsaysay Award. She funds and supervises two voluntary organisations: Navjyoti and India Vision Foundation. She holds a law degree and a doctorate in the field of drug abuse and domestic violence, is an author and the subject of various books and films.

'It is a poem which I used to recite in school.'

The City 2

You tell yourself: I'll be gone
To some other land, some other sea,
To a city far lovelier than this
Could ever have been or hoped to be
Where every step now tightens the noose:
A heart in a body buried and out of use:
How long, how long must I be here
Confined among these dreary purlieus
Of the common mind? Wherever now I look
Black ruins of my life rise into view.
So many years have I been here
Spending and squandering, and nothing gained.
There's no new land, my friend, no
New sea; for the city will follow you,
In the same streets you'll wander endlessly,

The same mental suburbs slip from youth to age,
In the same house go white at last
The city is a cage.
No other places, always this
Your earthly landfall, and no ship exists
To take you from yourself. Ah don't you see
Just as you've ruined your life in this
One plot of ground you've ruined its worth
Everywhere now over the whole earth?

C. P. Cavafy

Contributed By:

Mani Shankar Aiyar - has played an active role as a Congressman and Member of Parliament. One of India's most well-known commentators and also an eminent columnist, he was a close friend and adviser to the late Rajiv Gandhi, and a former career diplomat in the Indian Foreign Service.

'While it is a poem of deep despair, it gives the one message, which, if understood, is the only way of raising oneself by the boot-straps from one's own despair: "No ship exists, to take you from yourself".'

The palace where Jamshid held his cup
The doe and the fox now rest and sup
Bahram who hunted game non-stop
Was hunted by death when his time was up.

I resolve daily that at dusk I shall repent
For a night with a cup full of wine spent.
In the presence of flowers, my resolve simply went
In such company, I only regret that I ever resolved to repent.

Khayam, if you are intoxicated with wine, enjoy!
If you are seated with a lover of thine, enjoy!
In the end, the Void the whole world employ
Imagine thou art not, while waiting in line, enjoy!

O friend, for the morrow let us not worry
This moment we have now, let us not hurry
When our time comes, we shall not tarry
With seven thousand-year-olds, our burden carry.
In childhood we strove to go to school,
Our turn to teach, joyous as a rule
The end of the story is sad and cruel
From dust we came, and gone with winds cool.

At dawn came a calling from the tavern
Hark drunken mad man of the cavern
Arise; let us fill with wine one more turn
Before destiny fills our cup, our urn.

If my coming were up to me, I'd never be born
And if my going were of my accord, I'd go with scorn
Isn't it better that in this world, so old and worn
Never to be born, neither stay, nor be away torn?

When the canary made its way to the field
Found the rose and wine smiling, kneeled,
In tongues its message in my ear it thus reeled
Hark, no moment in time did twice yield.

Heaven is incomplete without a heavenly romance
Let a glass of wine be my present circumstance
Take what is here now, let go of a promised chance
A drumbeat is best heard from a distance.

The day the stallion of time was tamed and trained
Venus and Jupiter were adorned and stained
This life for us was allotted and ordained
This was not our will; were thus chained and restrained.

The caravan of life shall always pass
Beware that is fresh as sweet young grass
Let's not worry about what tomorrow will amass
Fill my cup again, this night will pass, alas.
Happily I walked with the tavern down the line
Passed an old drunk, holding a bottle of wine
'Do you not fear God?' was reproach of mine
said, 'Mercy is God's sign, in silence I wine and dine.'

It is a day neither hot nor cold,
Clouds help the dry flowers unfold
The canary with his song to the flower told

Drink while you can, yourself don't scold.
This Old World we've named Cosmos by mistake
Is the graveyard of nights & days, no more awake
And a feast that hundred Jamshids did break
And a throne that hundred Bahrams did make.
The secrets eternal neither you know nor I
And answers to the riddle neither you know nor I
Behind the veil there is much talk about us, why
When the veil falls, neither you remain nor I.

Before time takes you by surprise
Ask for good red wine and get wise
You are not of gold, don't believe the lies
You are put to dust, once again you'll rise.

I brought the cup to my lips with greed
Begging for longevity, my temporal need
The cup brought its to mine, its secret did feed
Time never returns, drink, of this take heed.

All my companions, one by one died
With the Angel of Death they now reside
In the banquette of life the same wine we tried
A few cups ago, they fell to the side.
As the rising Venus and moon in the skies appear
To the goodness of quality wine, nothing comes near
I am amazed at the vendors of a liquid so dear
Where they'll buy a better thing, is not clear.

Don't permit sorrow to be your friend
Or let sadness and pain become your trend
Don't let the book or the farm you tend
Rule your life before to earth you descend.

Some in deep thought spirit seek
Some lost in awe, of doubt reek
I fear the voice, hidden but not weak
Cry out 'Awake! Both ways are oblique.'

Like God, if this world I could control
Eliminating the world would be my role
I would create the world anew, whole
Such that the free soul would attain desired goal.

This cup was made by the wise Lord
With love & care to the heights soared
The potter who shaped with such accord
To make and break the same clay, can also afford.

Signs of destiny have always been
Those hands inscribed both good and mean
What was written, came from the unseen
Though we tried without and worried within.

At all times, merrily try
To drink wine and in song cry
Millions of kings in silence lie
From coming of January and passing of July.

Drinking wine is my travail
Till my body is dead and stale
At my grave site all shall hail
The odor of wine shall prevail.

When the clay into a cup is molded
Its breaking, the drunk scolded;
Many limbs and heads are enfolded
Through whose love unfolded, by which decree folded?

Good and evil, our moral prison,
Joy and sorrow passing like seasons,
Fate in the way of logic and reason
Is the victim of far worse treason.
Lover of drunk and the outcast
Better than pious prayer and fast
Thou art the first and art the last
Caress if thou wilt, if thou wilt blast.

When the Maker formed nature
Why imperfect was the venture
If it is good, why departure
And if bad, why form capture?

This universal wheel, this merry-go-round
In our imagination we have found
The sun a flame, in the cosmic lantern bound
We are mere ghosts, revolving, the flame surround.

The rose claimed to be Jacob of grass and dirt
A red ruby resurrected with a green skirt
I said if this is so, show a sign of your hurt
Said just take a look at my bloody shirt.

Anxiously I began this course
With life my awe grew even worse
Unwillingly returned with force
What was the point, I ask my source.

In the wheel of fortune the unseen vine
Drink, be merry, wait your turn in line
When it is your turn, neither cry nor whine
Everyone must taste the same deadly wine.

O Life, you put many traps in my way
Dare to try, is what you clearly say
All that is, thy command must obey
You lead me away and call me astray.
Why treat thy slave so cold as ice?
Where is thy light to save me from vice?
Even with command of Paradise
Where is thy gift above my just price?
They say in heaven are beautiful lovers
Sweet taste of wine in the air hovers
Fear not if succumbed to same earthly powers
In the end the same, one discovers.

Take all the worldly goods, but in lieu
Let the beauty of nature renew
And at night on the grass like dew
And in the morn take me away from view.

Drink wine that drives away joy and pain
And the thought of Seventy Two nations' reign
Never withhold from such elixir again
Of which one sip will purge all that's insane.

Hark! Feed me wine, if you really care
Turn into ruby my face of amber
Bathe me in wine when death me ensnare
With boards of vine my coffin bear.

An old potter at his wheel
Clay and dirt mould and deal
My inner eye would reveal
My father's dust bears his seal.

Once transpired, cannot be changed
Only pain will come if remorse engaged
Though with sorrow you may be aged
Not even a dot will be rearranged.
Each drop of wine that is spilt
Burnt deep in my heart and sorrow built
I drink wine while prayer thou wilt
The water that quenched the fire of my guilt
Alas the youthful fire is a dying ember
The spring of life has reached December
What is termed youth, I vaguely remember
But know not whence and how from life's chamber.

In the cosmic game of polo you are the ball
The mallet's left and right becomes your call
He who causes your movements, your rise and fall
He is the one, the only one, who knows it all.

From the depths of earth to heights of Saturn
We've solved all riddles, turn after turn
Break every chain, our ignorance burn
Except the riddle that fills the urn.

Tonight I shall embrace a gallon cup
With at least two cups of wine I'll sup
I'll divorce my mind and religion stop
With daughter of vine, all night I'll stay up

Wherever you go in the land of God
Flowers bloom from kingly blood
Violet with its colorful shroud
Was a beauty mole on a face once proud.

Beloved friends let us gather
For each other, together care
With raised cups salute and share
In memory of he who isn't there.
The grass that grows by every stream
Like angelic smiles faintly gleam
Step gently, cause it not to scream
For it has grown from a lover's dream.
Those who went in pursuit of knowledge
Soared up so high, stretched the edge
Were still encaged by the same dark hedge
Brought us some tales ere life to death pledge.

Once upon a time, in a potter's shop
I saw two thousand clay pot and cup
Suddenly a lone pot cried out, 'stop!
Where the vendor, buyer, where my prop?'

We are the puppets and fate the puppeteer
This is not a metaphor, but a truth sincere
On this stage, fate for sometime our moves steer
Into the chest of non-existence, one by one disappear.

The signs of what's to come has always been
Has always written both benevolent and mean
What is our lot was given by the hand unseen
With futility we try, exert, weep or keen

This clay pot like a lover once in heat
A lock of hair his senses did defeat
The handle that has made the bottleneck its own seat
Was once the embrace of a lover that entreat.

The sun with its morning light the earth ensnare
The king celebrated the day with a wine so fair
The herald of dawn intoxicated would blare
Its fame and aroma, for time having not a care.

Omar Khayyam

Contributed By:

M.J. Akbar - is the founder and editor-in-chief of India's first global newspaper, the *Asian Age*. He is a distinguished journalist, celebrated author and has been a socio-political commentator through his writing.

'It spans the human experience, with man both as the centre of a vast universe as well as a dot upon a timeless creation.'

From *The Lay of the Last Minstrel* 4

Breathes there the man with soul so dead
Who never to himself hath said,
This is my own, my native land!
Whose heart hath ne'er within him burn'd,
As home his footsteps he hath turn'd
From wandering on a foreign strand!
If such there breathe, go, mark him well;
For him no Minstrel raptures swell;

High though his titles, proud his name,
Boundless his wealth as wish can claim
Despite those titles, power, and pelf,
The wretch, concentered all in self,
Living, shall forfeit fair renown,
And, doubly dying, shall go down
To the vile dust, from whence he sprung,
Unwept, unhonored, and unsung.

Sir Walter Scott

Contributed By:

Dr P. C. Alexander - was the governor of Maharashtra and former Indian high commissioner to London. Dr Alexander was also nominated for the post of the president of India.

'In a few lines he has brought out the intensity of his feelings of love for his country. I consider this as one of the best poems on the concept of patriotism.'

Let your life come amongst them like a flame of light, my child,
unflickering and pure, and delight them into silence.

They are cruel in their greed and their envy,
their words are like hidden knives thirsting for blood.

Go and stand amidst their scowling hearts, my child,
and let your gentle eyes fall upon them like the
forgiving peace of the evening over the strife of the day.

Let them see your face, my child, and thus know the
meaning of all things, let them love you and love each other.

Come and take your seat in the bosom of the limitless, my child.
At sunrise open and raise your heart like a blossoming flower, and
at sunset bend your head and in silence
complete the worship of the day.

Rabindranath Tagore

Contributed By:

Tina Ambani - is the guiding force behind *Harmony*, the annual show that is a platform for art. She has tied up with the NGO, Aseema Foundation, which rehabilitates and educates street children. The ex-actress is married to industrialist Anil Ambani.

'Like all great poetry, this poem is simple, inspiring and touching. I love the unique blend of depth, sentiment and rhythm in Rabindranath Tagore's poetry. He remains my favourite poet'.

The Poem 6

Can it be true that I forget you?

We haste on heedless, forgetting
The flowers on the roadside hedge

Yet they breathe unaware of their
Forgetfulness, feeling it with music

You come to me with the first
Ray of dawn and I lost you
With last gold of the evening

And ever since I am finding you
Through the dark - no, no
You are no mere picture.

Rabindranath Tagore

Contributed By:

Baba Amte - was born to a family of jagirdars. He trained in law, before deciding to dedicate his life to social justice. Baba Amte has devoted his life to the care and rehabilitation of leprosy patients, even offering his body for experiments to grow leprosy germs. He used his honours and awards, amounting to Rs 5 million, to run his Anandavan Ashram, set up to dispel prejudice against leprosy victims. In 1999, he was awarded the Gandhi Peace Prize for his work with the leprosy afflicted, and his concept of 'Shramik Vidyapeeth', where patients and volunteers work together. To establish peace and raise environmental consciousness, Baba Amte launched the Bharat Jodo (Unite India) Movement.

'Rabindranath Tagore had sent this poem to me with signature in his own handwriting. The poem is special for me because it has inspired me to find him through the dark for so many decades. Yet they breathe unaware of their forgetfulness feeling it with music. It has inspired me and my inmates at Anandwan. Inspiration always motivates. It should not be analysed. It has helped me to detect minutest vibrations of human temperament.'

Daffodils 7

I wander'd lonely as a cloud
That floats on high o'er vales and hills,
When all at once I saw a crowd,
A host, of golden daffodils;
Beside the lake, beneath the trees,
Fluttering and dancing in the breeze.

Continuous as the stars that shine
And twinkle on the Milky Way,
They stretch'd in never-ending line
Along the margin of a bay:
Ten thousand saw I at a glance,
Tossing their heads in sprightly dance.

The waves beside them danced; but they
Out-did the sparkling waves in glee:
A poet could not but be gay,
In such a jocund company:
I gazed-and gazed-but little thought
What wealth the show to me had brought:

For oft, when on my couch I lie
In vacant or in pensive mood,
They flash upon that inward eye
Which is the bliss of solitude;
And then my heart with pleasure fills,
And dances with the daffodils.

William Wordsworth

Contributed By:

Mulk Raj Anand - the late novelist was a short-story writer and art critic. He wrote books on art history and also published books on subjects as diverse as Marx and Engels in India, Tagore, Nehru, Aesop's Fables, the Kama Sutra, erotic sculpture, and Indian ivories. He is frequently referred to as one of the 'founding fathers' of the Indian English novel.

'It conveys man's sense of joy in nature.'

Vishwanathan Anand - It is impossible to summarize Vishwanathan Anand, India's foremost chess master, in a paragraph. He became an International Master at the age of fourteen-the youngest Asian to achieve that distinction. His efforts won him the Arjuna Award, and in 1987, he became India's first Grandmaster. Vishwanathan also holds the distinction of being the World Rapid Chess Champion. This winner of the World Chess Title is a source of inspiration to aspiring chess talent in the country.

Karan Johar - is a leading film director and producer in Indian cinema with box-office triumphs such as *Kabhi Khushi Khabhi Gham* and *Kuch Kuch Hota Hai* to his credit.

Where the Mind Is Without Fear 8

Where the mind is without fear and the head is held high;
Where knowledge is free;
Where the world has not been broken up into fragments
By narrow domestic walls;
Where words come out from the depth of truth;
Where tireless striving stretches its arms towards perfection
Where the clear stream of reason has not lost its way
Into the dreary desert sand of dead habit
Where the mind is led forward by thee
Into ever-widening thought and action—
Into that heaven of freedom, my Father, let my country awake.

Rabindranath Tagore

Contributed By:

Tariq Ansari - is the managing director of Mid-Day Multimedia. An MBA from Notre Dame University, USA, his personal interests include ceramics, carpets, calligraphy and crime fiction.

'From the very first time I heard the poem, I was struck by the poet's wish for our country beyond narrow parochial nationalism.'

Rahul Bajaj - is an eminent industrialist and the chairman and managing director of Bajaj Auto Ltd. He is also the chairman of IIT, Mumbai, a post appointed by the president of India, and was recently appointed to the Rajya Sabha.

'This poem is special for me partly because it's by a great Indian. It articulates timeless ideals that strike a deep chord inside me. More so, when the reality around is quite the obverse. It provides part of the moral sustenance to live through the night and to work for tomorrow.'

Nana Chudasama - is the former mayor of Mumbai and president of the 'I Love Mumbai' committee. The ex-sheriff is also the world chairman of Giant's International, a service organization that works towards the betterment of society and the upliftment of the poor and underprivileged.

'It is a very inspiring message.'

Aamir Khan - is one of India's most popular actors. The method actor has performed in all genres of films, earning critical acclaim at home and internationally. *Lagaan* was nominated for an Oscar in the best foreign film category. He was once the state tennis champion of Maharashtra. Aamir Khan was offered the Padma Bhushan in 2003.

Anand Patwardhan - is an activist and award-winning documentary film-maker. His films have explored subjects like communal violence and patriarchy, the plight of slum dwellers and the nuclear issue. Many of his films were banned by state television channels in India and became the subject of litigation by the film-maker who successfully challenged the censorship rulings in court.

Aruna Roy - is a recipient of the Magsaysay Award for community leadership and international understanding. She was an IAS officer until 1974, but resigned to join the social work and research center in Tilonia, Rajasthan, set up by her husband Sanjit Roy. She set up the Mazdoor Kisan Shakti Sangathana, a working example of a transparent organisation. She is a strong supporter of the movement for the right to information.

'This speaks to us of the universal nature of knowledge. That the myopia of parochialism and narrow mindedness reduces all knowledge to tools of opportunism and oppression. It is of special significance to all of us in India today. The poem has been like a talisman for me, guiding me through difficult times.'

Prannoy Roy - began his television production house, NDTV in 1988 with his show *The World this Week* on Doordarshan. An economist, chartered accountant, author and psephologist, Mr Roy has worked as a consultant with the World Bank, the Asian Development Bank and the Economic Advisory Council of the Planning Commission. This commentator and anchorperson has also been the economic advisor to the ministry of finance and the government of India. Besides this, he has been president of the policy group on a macro-econometric short term forecasting model for India. He also has a doctorate from the Indian Institute of Management (Ahmedabad).

'Like Tagore, so many years ago, I too dream of India in these terms and do what I can to achieve this.'

Dr Mallika Sarabhai - is a leading exponent of Bharat Natyam and Kuchipudi. She is the co-director of the Darpan Academy of Performing Arts in Ahmedabad. The danseuse is also a noted film-maker, activist, TV anchor, editor and publisher and has earned a doctorate from the Indian Institute of Management (Ahmedabad).

Viren J. Shah - An alumnus of Harvard Business School, Viren Shah has juggled roles as governor of Bengal, veteran parliamentarian and industrialist. The chief of Mukand Group of Industries, he has headed several chambers of commerce.

'I find the poem inspires and has a permanent relevance. This poem reflects the yearning of the ages for a world in which there is opportunity for all for socio-economic and political equality.'

Dr Kiran Mazumdar Shaw - is the chairperson and managing director, Biocon India Ltd, and chairperson of the Confederation of Indian Industry (CII) national committee on biotechnology. She is also India's first woman brewmaster. She was awarded the Padma Shri in 1989.

'Tagore's poem truly inspires uninhibited, creative thinking with a deep sense of responsibility and conviction. This is so relevant to the knowledge business and scientific world that we live in but equally a strong reminder to the turbulent world that we live in today that is losing its sense of reason and harmony. It truly is an eternal poem.'

Kavita Krishnamurthy Subramaniam - is a versatile playback singer, and is happily married to violin virtuoso Dr L. Subramaniam. She spends her time between Mumbai, Bangalore (where she is now based) and the USA (where her husband lives for part of the year).

'I have great associations of my childhood attached to this poem as my father used to read this very often to us. I find the words very inspiring.'

मेरी आवाज़ सुनो 9

मेरी आवाज़ सुनो, प्यार का राज़ सुनो

मैंने इक फूल जो सीने पे सजा रखा था
उसके परदे में तुम्हें दिल से लगा रखा था
था जुदा सबसे मेरे इश्क़ का अंदाज़ सुनो
मेरी आवाज़ सुनो, प्यार का राज़ सुनो
मेरी आवाज़ सुनो, प्यार का राज़ सुनो

ज़िंदगी-भर मुझे नफ़रत-सी रही अश्कों से
मेरे ख़्वाबों को तुम अश्कों में डुबोते क्यों हो
जो मेरी तरह जिया करते हैं कब मरते हैं
थक गया हूँ, मुझे सो लेने दो, रोते क्यों हो
सोके भी जागते ही रहते हैं, जाँबाज़, सुनो
मेरी आवाज़ सुनो, प्यार का राज़ सुनो

मेरी दुनिया में न पूरब है न पश्चिम कोई
सारे इनसान सिमट आए खुली बाँहों में
कल भटकता था मैं जिन राहों में तनहा-तनहा
क़ाफ़िले कितने मिले आज उन्हीं राहों में
और सब निकले मेरे हमदर्द-ओ-हमराज़ सुनो
मेरी आवाज़ सुनो, प्यार का राज़ सुनो

नौनिहाल आते हैं, अर्थी को किनारे कर लो
मैं जहाँ था, इन्हें जाना है वहाँ से आगे
आसमाँ इनका, ज़मीं इनकी, ज़माना इनका
हैं कई इनके जहाँ, मेरे जहाँ से आगे
इन्हें कलियाँ न कहो, ये हैं चमनसाज़, सुनो
मेरी आवाज़ सुनो, प्यार का राज़ सुनो

क्यों सँवारी है यह चंदन की चिता मेरे लिए
मैं कोई जिस्म नहीं हूँ कि जला दोगे मुझे

राख के साथ बिखर जाऊँगा मैं दुनिया में
तुम जहाँ खाओगे ठोकर वहीं पाओगे मुझे
हर क़दम पर है नए मोड़ का आग़ाज़, सुनो
मेरी आवाज़ सुनो, प्यार का राज़ सुनो

Hear My Voice

Hear my voice, hear, the secret of love

I've hidden my love for you
In the petals of a flower pinned close to my heart.
My love is different . . . listen
Hear my voice, hear, the secret of love
Hear my voice, hear, the secret of love

All my life I have detested sorrow
Why do you now drown my dreams in your tears?
Those who live as I have, do they die?
I am tired. Let me sleep. Do not weep.
The brave lie awake even in sleep, listen . . .
Hear my voice, hear, the secret of love

In my world, there is neither east nor west
My arms reach out to embrace all humanity.
The deserted roads I yesterday trod all alone
are full of caravans today
and all travelers are just like me
Hear my voice, hear, the secret of love

Set the bier aside; make way for the children
They have to go much further than I have.
Their worlds are many and far ahead of mine
Their is the sky, their the earth and the era
Don't call them flowerbuds; they are the gardeners
Hear my voice, hear, the secret of love

Why do you adorn my pyre with logs of sandalwood?
I am not just a body to be burnt away
I will be scattered with my ashes
And you will meet me each time you stumble
Remember, each step, each turn is a new beginning
Hear my voice, hear, the secret of love

Kaifi Azmi

Contributed By:

Shabana Azmi - After a film career spanning thirty-odd years, Shabana Azmi is an internationally acclaimed actress, member of the Rajya Sabha and social activist. She is the winner of an unprecedented five national awards for best actress (for roles in the films *Ankur*, *Khandar*, *Arth*, *Paar* and *Godmother*). As chairperson of Nivara Hakk Suraksha Samiti, Shabana Azmi arranged for land for the slum dwellers of the disputed Sanjay Gandhi Nagar slums in Mumbai. In 1988, she was awarded the Padma Shree by the government of India for her contributions to society. Shabana Azmi has recently been appointed the United Nations goodwill ambassador on population and development.

'This poem was written by my father, the late Urdu poet, Kaifi Azmi. For the film Naunihal, *directed by Sawan Kumar Tak.*

In the film, it is a voice over of Jawaharlal Nehru as his funeral procession is being taken through the streets thronging with weeping multitudes of people. However, it is a poem of hope because he believed that children hold the future in their hands.When my father passed away on 10th May, 2002, I sought solace in the poem as my father's message to our family.'

क्या भूलूं क्या याद करूं? 10

जीवन की आपाधापी में कब वक़्त मिला
कुछ देर कहीं पर बैठ कभी यह सोच सकूं,
जो किया, कहा, माना उसमें क्या बुरा-भला ।

जिस दिन मेरी चेतना जगी मैंने देखा
मैं खड़ा हुआ हूं इस दुनिया के मेले में,
हर एक यहाँ पर एक भुलावे में भूला,
हर एक लगा है अपनी-अपनी दे-ले में,
कुछ देर रहा हक्का-बक्का, भौचक्का-सा
आ गया कहाँ, क्या करूँ यहाँ, जाऊँ किस जा ?
फिर एक तरफ़ से आया ही तो धक्का-सा,
मैंने भी बहना शुरू किया उस रेले में;

यों बाहर की रेला-ठेली ही क्या कम थी,
जो भीतर भी भावों का ऊहापोह मचा,
जो किया, उसी को करने की मजबूरी थी,
जो कहा, वही मन के अन्दर से उबल चला.

जीवन की आपाधापी में कब वक़्त मिला
कुछ देर कहीं पर बैठ कभी यह सोच सकूं,
जो किया, कहा, माना उसमें क्या बुरा-भला ।

मेला जितना भड़कीला रंग-रंगीला था,
मानस के अन्दर उतनी ही कमज़ोरी थी,
जितना ज़्यादा संचित करने की ख़्वाहिश थी,
उतनी ही छोटी अपने कर की झोरी थी,
जितनी ही ठहरे रहने की थी अभिलाषा,
उतना ही रेले तेज़ ढकेले जाते थे,
क्रय-विक्रय तो ठण्डे दिल से हो सकता है,
यह तो भागा-भागा की छीना-छोरी थी,

अब मुझसे पूछा जाता है क्या बतलाऊँ,
क्या भान अकिंचन बिखराता पथ पर आया,
वह कौन रतन अतमोल मिला ऐसा मुझको,
जिस पर अपना मन-प्राण निछावर कर आया;

यह थी तक़दीरी बात मुझे गुण दोष न दो,
जिसको समझा था सोना, वह मिट्टी निकली।

जिसको समझा था आँसू, वह मोती निकला।
जीवन की आपाधापी में कब वक़्त मिला
कुछ देर कहीं पर बैठ कभी यह सोच सकूं,
जो किया, कहा, माना उसमें क्या बुरा-भला।

मैं कितना ही भूलूं, भटकूं य भरमाऊँ,
है एक कहीं मंजिल जो मुझे बुलाती है,
कितने ही मेरे पाँव पड़े ऊँचे-नीचे,
प्रतिपल वह मेरे पास चली ही आती है,
मुझ पर विधि का एहसान बहुत-सी बातों का
पर मैं कृतज्ञ उसका इस पर सबसे ज़्यादा
नभ ओले बरसाये, धरती शोले उगले,
अनवरत समय की चक्की चलती जाती है;

मैं जहाँ खड़ा था कल उस थल पर आज नहीं,
कल इसी जगह फिर पाना मुझको मुश्किल है;
ले मापदण्ड जिसकी परिवर्तित कर देतीं
केवल छूकर ही देश -काल की सीमाएँ

जग दे मुझ पर फ़ैसला उसे जैसा भाये
लेकिन मैं तो बेरोक सफ़र में जीवन के
इस एक और पहलू से होकर निकल चला।

जीवन की आपाधापी में कब वक़्त मिला

कुछ देर कहीं पर बैठ कभी यह सोच सकूं,
जो किया, कहा, माना उसमें क्या बुरा-भला ।

What Shall I Remember? What Shall I Forget?

Did I take the time, somewhere,
In the chaos of life, to sit and reflect on
The good or bad in what I did, said, accepted?

One day, there was an awakening.
And I saw myself on the fairground of the world
Every person there was lost in a dream
Every person absorbed in his own give and take
I stood there stunned and dumb asking
Where am I, what will I do here, where do I go when
A push from the crowd
Compelled me to go with the flow.

Was the chaos outside not enough that
It had to be reflected inside of me?
What I did, I was compelled to do,
What I said, erupted out of me.

Did I take the time, somewhere
In the chaos of life, to sit and reflect on
The good or bad in what I did, said, accepted?

The world was violently colourful
And equally drab the human soul
The size of the hands far too small, mocked
The limitless desire to hoard infinitely
The relentless push of the swelling crowd jeered

The ardent desire to stand still
Understanding can come only in a still mind
This was a continuous scramble.

What should I say when people ask me
Why I have taken this path
What precious gem have I found
On which to bestow my heart and soul?
This was my destiny, do not praise or condemn
What appeared to be gold turned out to be clay,
What I believed tears turned out to be pearls.

Did I take the time, somewhere
In the chaos of life, to sit and reflect on
The good or bad in what I did, said, accepted?

Much as I may forget, stray, delude myself
There is a goal somewhere that calls out to me
My steps may wander, yet every moment it inches closer to me.
Fortune has blessed me in many ways
But for this I owe her the most:
The heavens may rain hail, the earth may belch fire
Yet the wheel of time keeps turning eternally.

I am not where I was yesterday
It will be hard to find me here tomorrow
How do we assess constant evolution
Even as boundaries shift and change?

The world may judge me as it pleases
I am off, through one more aspect of
The untrammeled journey of my life

Did I take the time, somewhere
In the chaos of life, to sit and reflect on
The good or bad in what I did, said, accepted?

Harivansh Rai Bachchan

Contributed By:

Amitabh Bachchan - A luminary of Indian cinema, Amitabh Bachchan is a living, acting legend. His first movie was *Saat Zindagi* (1969) and in 1973, he was nicknamed 'The Angry Young Man' of Indian cinema after his role in *Zanjeer*. Mr Bachchan's versatility rapidly became a prototype for many rising stars - and he even did his own singing, sans playback! Born in Allahabad, to the poet Harivansh Rai Bachchan and Teji Bachchan, Amitabh Bachchan is probably India's busiest, most famed and most loved actor, with a host of films, including *Baghban*, *Khakee*, *Lakshya*, and the hit game show *Kaun Banega Crorepati* to his credit.

'This poem is very special to me because of the several occasions I had of listening to it, sung by my father at vast Kavi Sammellans and at private gatherings. It always evokes in me a great emotional bond between my father and myself. The poem was written during a very dark phase in my father's personal life. The words and its construction reflect that emotion.

In life the sun doesn't always shine. There are moments of darkness too and when mankind is burdened with unhappy moments, it becomes difficult for him what to forget and what to remember, because the intensity of both is so huge, that they weigh almost equally on the mind. This poem in particular expresses that dilemma, hence I am fond of it.'

If you can keep your head when all about you
Are losing theirs and blaming it on you;
If you can trust yourself when all men doubt you,
But make allowance for their doubting too;
If you can wait and not be tired by waiting,
Or, being lied about, don't deal in lies,
Or, being hated, don't give way to hating,
And yet don't look too good, nor talk too wise;
If you can dream-and not make dreams your master;
If you can think-and not make thoughts your aim;
If you can meet with Triumph and Disaster
And treat those two impostors just the same;
If you can bear to hear the truth you've spoken
Twisted by knaves to make a trap for fools,
Or watch the things you gave your life to, broken,
And stoop and build 'em up with worn-out tools,
If you can make one heap of all your winnings
And risk it all on one turn of the pitch-and-toss,
And lose, and start again at your beginnings
And never breathe a word about your loss;
If you can force your heart and nerve and sinew
To serve your turn long after they are gone,
And so hold on when there is nothing in you
Except the Will which says to them: 'Hold on!'

If you can talk with crowds and keep your virtue,
Or walk with kings-nor lose the common touch,
If neither foes nor loving friends can hurt you;
If all men count with you, but none too much,
If you can fill the unforgiving minute

With sixty seconds' worth of distance run,
Yours is the Earth and everything that's in it,
And – which is more – you'll be a Man, my son!

Rudyard Kipling

Contributed By:

Lord Bagri - the renowned UK based entrepreneur is the founder and patriarch of the Metdist group of companies. The first person of non-British origin to be the chairman of the London Metal Exchange (LME), he was awarded the title of 'Honorary President of the LME'. Lord Bagri was made Life Peer in 1997, further to his CBE in 1995.

'I like this poem because it conveys a message which is so sensible and profound.'

Farzana Contractor - is the CEO of the *Afternoon Despatch & Courier*. She is also the editor of *Upper Crust*, a wine, food and style magazine.

'It says it all. It stays in my mind constantly, urging me, inspiring me to live life according to Kipling's tough but awesome code.'

Rahul Dravid - is the captain of the Indian cricket team and a true stalwart in the cricketing world today. Nicknamed 'The Wall' because of the number of times he has saved the Indian team from imminent disaster, this right handed batsman remains calm and consistent even under pressure. His greatest ambition is to enable the Indian team to win the World Cup.

'It is a poem that I was given in my childhood and it was a huge inspiration. It carries a beautiful message on life.'

Adi Godrej - is chairman of the Godrej group. One of India's most distinguished business people, he has traveled to over seventy countries and is an adventure sports enthusiast.

'This poem is very special to me because Rudyard Kipling captures the essence of being a good person and a strong leader, very well.'

Parmeshwar Adi Godrej - Wife of Adi Godrej, Parmeshwar Godrej has hosted mega-fundraising events to champion the AIDS cause. The socialite and art aficionado also designs and decorates homes.

'It is a clarion call to be all that you can be.'

The Road Not Taken 12

Two roads diverged in a yellow wood,
And sorry I could not travel both
And be one traveler, long I stood
And looked down one as far as I could
To where it bent in the undergrowth;

Then took the other, as just as fair,
And having perhaps the better claim,
Because it was grassy and wanted wear;
Though as for that the passing there
Had worn them really about the same,

And both that morning equally lay
In leaves no step had trodden black.
Oh, I kept the first for another day!
Yet knowing how way leads on to way,
I doubted if I should ever come back.

I shall be telling this with a sigh
Somewhere ages and ages hence:
Two roads diverged in a wood, and I –
I took the one less traveled by,
And that has made all the difference.

Robert Frost

Contributed By:

Manvinder Singh (Vindi) Banga - is the ex CEO of HLL, a subsidiary of Unilever, and the largest consumer product company in India. In May 2005 he was elevated to the board of Unilever as head of the foods business (57 per cent of global revenue), the position he currently holds. A gold medalist from IIM Ahmedabad and IIT Delhi, he is on the boards and managing committees of trade and non-trade institutions, including the CII, the Indian School of Business, Hyderabad, and IIM, Ahmedabad.

'It is about living life positively making the choices we need to make all the time.'

Harsh Goenka - the scion of the Goenka family, is the chairman of the conglomerate RPG Group. The industrialist is also a great patron of the arts and supports emerging artists.

'Roads fascinate me as metaphors of change, of journeys, of partings, of adventure and of life itself. Personally, I feel, that even though there may be many layers of meanings and allusions in a poem, it is the literal, surface-reading that determines much of its merit. I like this poem for its alternating shades of simplicity and profundity.'

Uday Kotak - is the chairman and managing director of Kotak Mahindra Bank. An entrepreneurial banker, Uday Kotak has broken new ground in India and turned his financial services group into a bank. He is also a trained sitar player!

'Life is about making choices all the time. We constantly reflect about 'what if I had taken the other road'? The poem captures this essence beautifully'.

Azim Premji - held the reins of leadership at Wipro at the vulnerable age of twenty-one. Today, the IT Services Company he nurtured and grew, ranks among the top 100 technology companies in the world. Voted among the most powerful leaders internationally, he made a vital contribution as member of the Prime Minister's Advisory Committee for Information Technology in India. In 2001, he established the Azim Premji Foundation–a non-profit organisation with a vision to facilitate universal elementary education. The foundation presently covers over 5,000 rural schools.

'I like this poem because it is a beautifully simple evocation of life's choices.'

हिमालय के प्रति 13

मेरे नगपति ! मेरे विशाल !
साकार, दिव्य, गौरव विराट,
पौरुष के पूंजीभूत ज्वाल ।
मेरी जननी के हिम-किरीट,
मेरे भारत के दिव्य भाल ।
मेरे नगपति ! मेरे विशाल ।

युग-युग अजेय, निर्बन्ध, मुक्त
युग-युग गर्वोन्नत, नित महान,
निस्सीम व्योम में तान रहा
युग से किस महिमा का वितान ।

कैसी अखण्ड यह चिर-समाधि
यतिवर ! कैसा यह अमर ध्यान,
तू महाशून्य में खोज रहा
किस जटिल समस्या का निदान !
उलझन का कैसा विषम जाल,
मेरे नगपति ! मेरे विशाल !

ओ, मौन तपस्या-लीन यती
पल-भर को तो कर दृगोन्मेष,
रे ज्वालाओं से दग्ध विकल
है तड़प रहा पद पर स्वदेश ।

सुख सिन्धु पंचनद, ब्रह्मपुत्र
गङ्गा, यमुना की अमिय धार,
जिस पुण्यभूमि की ओर बही
तेरी विगलित करुणा उदार ।

जिसके द्वारों पर खड़ा क्रान्त
सीमापति ! तूने की पुकार,

'पद-दलित इसे करना पीछे,
पहले ले मेरा सिर उतार ।'

उस पुण्यभूमि पर आज तपी
रे आन पड़ा संकट कराल,
व्याकुल तेरे सुत तड़प रहे
डँस रहे चतुर्दिक् विविध व्याल ।
मेरे नगपति ! मेरे विशाल !

कितनी मणियाँ लुट गईं ! मिटा
कितना मेरा वैभव अशेष,
तू ध्यान-मग्न ही रहा, इधर
वीरान हुआ प्यारा स्वदेश ।

कितनी द्रुपदा के बाल खुले
कितनी कलियों का अन्त हुआ,
कह हृदय खोल चित्तौर ! यहाँ
कितने दिन ज्वाल-वसन्त हुआ ।

पूछे, सिकता-कण से हिमपति
तेरा वह राजस्थान कहाँ ?
वन-वन स्वतन्त्रता-दीप लिये
फिरने वाला बलवान कहाँ ?

तू पूछ अवध से, राम कहाँ
वृन्दा ! बोलो, घनश्याम कहाँ ?
ओ मगध ! कहाँ मेरे अशोक
वह चन्द्रगुप्त बलधाम कहाँ ?

पैरों पर ही है पड़ी हुई
मिथिला भिखारिणी सुकुमारी,
तू पूछ, कहाँ इसने खोई
अपनी अनन्त निधियाँ सारी ।

री कपिलवस्तु ! कह बुद्धदेव
के वे मंगल उपदेश कहाँ ?
तिब्बत, इरान, जापान चीन
तक गये हुए सन्देश कहाँ ?

वैशाली के भग्नावशेष से
पूछ लिच्छवी - शान कहाँ ?
ओ री उदास गंडकी ! बता
विद्यापति कवि के गान कहाँ ?

तू मौन त्यागकर पूछ आज
बंगाल, नवाबी ताज कहाँ ?
भारत का अन्तिम ज्योति-नयन
मेरा प्यारा सीराज कहाँ ?

तु तरुण देश से पूछ अरे
गूँजा कैसा यह ध्वंस-राग ?
अम्बुधि अन्तस्तल बीच छिपी ?
यह सुलग रही है कौन आग ?

प्राची के प्रांगण बीच देख
जल रहा स्वर्ण-युग अग्निज्वाल,
तू सिंहनाद कर जाग यती ।
मेरे नगपति ! मेरे विशाल !

रे रोक युधिष्ठिर को न यहाँ
जाने दे उनको स्वर्ग धीर,
पर फिरा हमें गांडीव, गदा
लौटा दे अर्जुन, भीम वीर ।

कह दे शंकर से आज करें
वे प्रलय-नृत्य फिर एक बार,
सारे भारत में गूँज उठे

'हर हर बम' का फिर 'महोच्चार ।

ले अँगड़ाई उठ, हिले धरा
कर निज विराट स्वर में निनाद,
तू शैलराट् ! हुंकार भरे
फट जाय कुहा, भागे प्रमाद ।

तू मौन त्याग, कर सिंहनाद
रे तपी ! आज तप का न काल,
नवयुग शंखध्वनि जगा रही
तू जाग, जाग, मेरे विशाल !

मेरी जननी के हिम किरीट
मेरे भारत के दिव्य भाल,
नवयुग शंखध्वनि जगा रही
जागे नगपति ! जागे विशाल ।

रामधारीसिंह 'दिनकर'

Ode to the Himalayas

My towering inspiration! O endless one!
Majestic, radiant, proud, immovable,
Protector of our past glory
My motherland's crown of snow
O glittering shield of Bharat
My towering inspiration! O endless one!

Unconquerable over centuries
You stand unobstructed, honoured one.
Your infinite greatness stretches the distance
Miraculous guardian of the wealth of ages.

O great one, explain this unending trance
This endless meditation
You search the eternal void
For which conundrum do you seek an answer
In an intricate web of confusion?
My towering inspiration! O endless one!

O silent sacrifice, lost in thought
Open your eyes for a moment
Raging flames besiege the country
As independence struggles
For every step.

The ever flowing joyful Sindhu, the five rivers,
Brahmaputra, Ganga, Yamuna
They bless our virtuous land wherever they flow
From your generosity and compassion.

Whenever we face a threat
You stand guard like a general in command
Whenever we have summoned help
Before we lose our honour
All foes are crushed at your feet.

Our sacred land is aflame
Problems abound
Our sons are under attack
Form various directions
My towering inspiration! O endless one!

How many fortunes we have lost
How much of our culture has vanished
But you have been lost in contemplation
While my beloved country becomes powerless.

How many women have been widowed
How much of our culture has vanished
But you have been lost in contemplation
While my beloved country becomes powerless.

How many women have been widowed
How many youth have died in bloom
Open your heart and relate
How often flames have been lit
From where do they spring?

If you were asked, O Himalaya,
Where is your kingdom
Where is the mighty fight for freedom
That wandered from place to place?

Ask Avadh, 'Where is Ram'?
Ask Vrindavan, 'Where is Ghyansham'?
O Magadha, 'Where is my Asoka'?
'Where is the courageous Chandragupta'?

At your feet stands the princess Mithila
Stricken with poverty
Ask how she lost
Her boundless wealth.

Buddha asks: O Kapilavastu,
Where are the teaching of peace we spread
The messages we sent
To Tibet, Iran, Japan, China?

Ask Lichchavi
Where Vaishali's grandeur has gone
Ask dejected Gandaki
Where the songs of the poet Vidyapathi have gone.

Give up your silence today,
Ask Bengal: Where is the throne of Nawabs?
Where is my dear Siraj
The last light of Bharat's eyes?

Ask this young country
How this destructive note did reverberate
Buried deep in the mind of youth
Which fire is simmering in their hearts?

Witness the ancient ages
Of golden rule burning away

Wake up
Get to your feet like a lion
My towering inspiration! on endless one!

Now do not stop Yudhistir
Let him proceed to heaven
But return the bow and mace
And Arjun and the brave Bheem.

Tell Shankar to perform
The dance of destruction today
Let the country resound
With chants of praise to Him.

Wake up! Shake yourself! Sound the trumpets!
Use your powerful voice
Announce the call to battle
Disperse the fog of delusion.

Renounce your silence
Roar like a lion
End your meditation now.
The sound of the conch shell
Rouses the new age.
Wake up! Wake up! O endless one!

O snow crown of all ages
O glittering shield of Bharat
The sound of the conch shell
Rouses the new age.
My towering inspiration! O endless one!

Ramdhari Singh 'Dinkar'

Contributed By:

L. K. Advani - was the president of the Bharatiya Janata Party (BJP) until the end of 2005 and is leader of the opposition in the 14th Lok Sabha. He is a prominent figure in his party and was previously the deputy prime minister and home minister between 1998 and 2004. Perhaps his greatest mark in politics was during his tenure as the information and broadcasting minister in the Janata government. In 1977, he freed the media from legislative and executive fetters and institutionalised reforms. Thus, he eliminated press censorship and revoked anti-press legislation.

Epitaph on a Tyrant 14

Perfection, of a kind, was what he was after,
And the poetry he invented was easy to understand;
He knew human folly like the back of his hand,
And was greatly interested in armies and fleets;
When he laughed, respectable senators burst with laughter,
And when he cried the little children died in the streets.

W. H. Auden

Contributed By:

Shyam Benegal - Born in Hyderabad, Shyam Benegal is one of India's most acclaimed film-makers. His initiation into the world of feature films was through advertising. In a career spanning three decades, he invented what has come to be called 'middle cinema': his feature films include *Ankur, Manthan, Bhoomika, Junoon,* and *Zubeidaa*. He has directed a fifty-three episode television documentary, based on Jawaharlal Nehru's *Discovery of India*. One of his recent endeavours in the direction of documentary films is a cinematic study of the early years of Gandhi in South Africa called *The Making of the Mahatma*. He has been the chairman of the Film and Television Institute of India and was conferred the Padma Bhushan. Shyam Benegal is an influential presence in Indian and international film circles.

'Did Auden have a crystal ball, or was he clairvoyant? His poems, written in the 1930s and '40s, as a shocked reaction to the World Wars, are eerily, unintentionally, prophetic. This chilling verse, an Auden classic, speaks of the defeated and the victorious. Humanity's evil face exudes in the last two lines-the dictator, the approving laughter from sycophants, and the cry for death. His poems should be read as warnings-the price of humanity is eternal vigilance.'

Lead Kindly Light 15

Lead, Kindly Light, amid th' encircling gloom,
    Lead Thou me on!
The night is dark and I am far from home—
    Lead Thou me on!
Keep Thou my feet; I do not ask to see
The distant scene,—one step enough for me.

I was not ever thus, nor pray'd that Thou
    Shouldst lead me on.
I loved to choose and see my path; but now
    Lead Thou me on!
I loved the garish day, and, spite of fears,
Pride ruled my will: remember not past years.

So long Thy power hath blest me, sure it still
    Will lead me on,
O'er moor and fen, o'er crag and torrent, till
    The night is gone;
And with the morn, those angel faces smile,
Which I have loved long since, and lost awhile.

Cardinal Newman

Contributed By:

Ela R. Bhatt - A former lawyer and social worker from a well-to-do family, Ela Bhatt launched the Self Employed Women's Association (SEWA) in 1972. It is the largest primary labour union in the country, representing a quarter of a million self-employed workers. She was nominated by the president of India to be a member of the Rajya Sabha. She was a member of the planning commission of India and chairperson and founder-member of Women's World Banking.

'I like the poem as it leads me to the path of light in my private and public life: "one step is enough for me" is my favourite line that has kept me humble and assured on the walk of my life.'

Shine Like a Star 16

When you'll see you have nothing to change in your fear,
When your dreams will come true through the trouble and grief,
Then you will shine like a star, be the best you can be
In your heart, in your life, in your dreams.
Share all your shine with the entire world,
Make the people believe in love.
In that time when you will shine like a star,
You will see the path you've chosen in your life.
And no one can stop your shine.
No one can stop you again.
It's your time.

Shine like a star, be the best you can be
In your heart, in your life, in your dreams.
Share all your shine with the entire world,
Make the people believe in love
Then you'll throw away your sadness,
Then you'll find again all your happiness.
Then you'll keep forever your kindness.
You will never be sad or brightless.
Shine like a star in the sky,
Shine like a star through the night.

Contributed By:

Subhash Chandra - is chairman and managing director of Zee Telefilms Limited and the promoter of Essel Group of Companies. His leading businesses include television networks, filmed entertainment, cable systems, satellite communications, theme parks, and online gaming. The one-time rice packer from Haryana has emerged as a media moghul with India's first Hindi language satellite channel.

'Through this poem it shows us how we can shine through all our troubles and griefs, just like the rainbow that shines through the rain.'

Faery Song 17

Shed no tear! O, shed no tear!
The flower will bloom another year.
Weep no more! O, weep no more!
Young buds sleep in the root's white core.
Dry your eyes! O dry your eyes!
For I taught in paradise.
To ease my breast of melodies,
Shed no tear.

Overhead! Look overhead!
'Mong the blossoms white and red,-
Look up, look up! I flutter now
On this fresh pomegranate bough.

See me! 'Tis this silvery bill
Ever cures the good man's ill,
Shed no tear! O, shed no tear!
The flower will bloom another year.
Adieu, adieu-I fly-adieu!
Adieu, adieu!

John Keats

Contributed By:

Justice Y. V. Chandrachud - was the longest serving chief justice of India in the country's Supreme Court. Importantly, he was chief justice during the emergency of 1975-1977.

'It shows how and why it is always good to hope for the best.'

इन्तज़ार 18

चाँद मद्धम है आसमाँ चुप है
नींद की गोद में जहाँ चुप है

दूर वादी में दूधिया बादल
झुक के पर्बत को प्यार करता है
दिल में नाकाम हसरतें ले कर
हम तेरा इंतज़ार करते हैं

इन बहारों के साये में आ जा
फिर मोहब्बत जवाँ रहे ना रहे
ज़िन्दगी तेरे नामुरादों पर
कल तलक मेहरबाँ रहे ना रहे

रोज़ की तरह आज भी तारे
सुबह की गर्द में ना खो जायें
आ तेरे ग़म में जागती आँखें
कम से कम एक रात सो जायें

चाँद मद्धम है आसमाँ चुप है
नींद की गोद में जहाँ चुप है

साहिर लुधियानवी

Waiting

The moon is dim, the sky is silent
The world is quiet in the lap of sleep

A milky cloud in a faraway valley
Reaches down to caress the mountain
Heart heavy with unrequited love
I wait for you

Come soon to me in the spring
Before love grows old
Or life grows tired of
The vanquished victims of your love

Like everyday, let not the stars
Vanish today in the dust of the morning
Come, give eyes heavy with the sleeplessness of your grief
At least a night of rest

The moon is dim, the sky is silent
The world is quiet in the lap of sleep

Saahir Ludhianvi

Contributed By:

Yash Chopra - The Lahore born Yash Chopra is one of India's leading film directors whose cinematic acumen surpasses that of any other. He founded his own production house, Yash Raj Films, in 1970. For forty years, he has made films that break with tradition: besides *Lamhe*, *Parampara* and the hugely successful *Darr*, he created *Dil To Pagal Hai.* Critics say the last was defining, blazing a new visual and cinematic style in Bollywood. He has won many awards including the prestigious Dadasaheb Phalke Award, for his contribution to Indian cinema. The film *Dilwale Dulhania Le Jaenge*, directed by his older son, Aditya, enhanced producer Yash Chopra's position as a leading patron of the Indian commercial film.

'This poem is very close to my heart and is my foremost favourite, written by my favourite poet Sahir Ludhianvi. Every line of this poem gives the visuals in the mind of the poet. It reflects the haunting quality of the poetry and a very romantic feeling. It's a poem of longing love and life.'

Patterns 19

I walk down the garden-paths,
And all the daffodils
Are blowing, and the bright blue squills.
I walk down the patterned garden-paths
In my stiff, brocaded gown.
With my powdered hair and jewelled fan,
I too am a rare
Pattern. As I wander down
The garden paths.
My dress is richly figured,
And the train
Makes a pink and silver stain
On the gravel, and the thrift
Of the borders.
Just a plate of current fashion,
Tripping by in high-heeled, ribboned shoes.
Not a softness anywhere about me,
Only whalebone and brocade.
And I sink on a seat in the shade
Of a lime tree. For my passion
Wars against the stiff brocade.
The daffodils and squills
Flutter in the breeze
As they please.
And I weep;
For the lime-tree is in blossom
And one small flower has dropped upon my bosom.

And the splashing of waterdrops
In the marble fountain

Comes down the garden-paths.
The dripping never stops.
Underneath my stiffened gown
Is the softness of a woman bathing in a marble basin,
A basin in the midst of hedges grown
So thick, she cannot see her lover hiding,
But she guesses he is near,
And the sliding of the water
Seems the stroking of a dear
Hand upon her.
What is Summer in a fine brocaded gown!
I should like to see it lying in a heap upon the ground.
All the pink and silver crumpled up on the ground.

I would be the pink and silver as I ran along the paths,
And he would stumble after,
Bewildered by my laughter.
I should see the sun flashing from his sword-hilt and the buckles on his shoes.
I would choose
To lead him in a maze along the patterned paths,
A bright and laughing maze for my heavy-booted lover,
Till he caught me in the shade,
And the buttons of his waistcoat bruised my body as he clasped me,
Aching, melting, unafraid.
With the shadows of the leaves and the sundrops,
And the plopping of the waterdrops,
All about us in the open afternoon–
I am very like to swoon
With the weight of this brocade,
For the sun sifts through the shade.

Underneath the fallen blossom
In my bosom,
Is a letter I have hid.
It was brought to me this morning by a rider from the Duke.
'Madam, we regret to inform you that Lord Hartwell
Died in action Thursday se' nnight.'
As I read it in the white, morning sunlight,

The letters squirmed like snakes.
'Any answer, Madam,' said my footman.
'No,' I told him.
'See that the messenger takes some refreshment.
No, no answer.'
And I walked into the garden,
Up and down the patterned paths,
In my stiff, correct brocade.
The blue and yellow flowers stood up proudly in the sun,
Each one.
I stood upright too,
Held rigid to the pattern
By the stiffness of my gown.
Up and down I walked,
Up and down.

In a month he would have been my husband.
In a month, here, underneath this lime,
We would have broke the pattern;
He for me, and I for him,
He as Colonel, I as Lady,
On this shady seat.
He had a whim
That sunlight carried blessing.
And I answered, 'It shall be as you have said.'
Now he is dead.

In Summer and in Winter I shall walk
Up and down
The patterned garden-paths
In my stiff, brocaded gown.
The squills and daffodils
Will give place to pillared roses, and to asters, and to snow.
I shall go
Up and down,
In my gown.
Gorgeously arrayed,
Boned and stayed.
And the softness of my body will be guarded from embrace
By each button, hook, and lace.
For the man who should loose me is dead,
Fighting with the Duke in Flanders,
In a pattern called a war.
Christ! What are patterns for?

Amy Lowell

Contributed By:

Charles Correa - Architect, planner, activist and theoretician, Charles Correa has emerged as a major figure in contemporary architecture worldwide. His work covers a wide range, from the Mahatma Gandhi Memorial at the Sabarmati Ashram to the Jawahar Kala Kendra in Jaipur and the State Assembly for Madhya Pradesh.

'This is indeed an extraordinary poem. Not just for the pacifist values it so brilliantly conveys, but also for the mood it generates. Read it twice. You'll realise how powerful are the patterns that, consciously or not, control us as human beings.The very same pattern seeming to suffocate us and at the very next moment, becoming a life-support vital to our survival.

The whole poem is as exquisitely constructed as one of Mozart's minuets. The garden like its occupant, is fastidious, controlled, manicured to perfection. The ambience gets more and more oppressive till we ultimately reach that final, shattering cry.'

A Farewell 20

Be good, sweet maid, and let who will be clever.
Do noble things, not dream them all day long,
And you will make of life and death together
One grand sweet song.

Anonymous

Contributed By:

Gerson da Cunha - is a veteran adman, theatre personality, activist and social commentator. As an activist, he is the founder-member of Bombay First and also the convener of AGNI. Gerson has published a book of poetry and has been communication advisor at UNICEF. He is also an active trustee of CRY - Child Rights and You.

'This poem was quoted to us by the inspector of schools when we were leaving St Mary's, Bombay, on the threshold of the wicked world.'

Children's Eyes 21

What kind of world is it my friend
that little children see?
I wonder if they see God first
because they just believe?

Do they see strength in caring eyes
that watch them as they play,
Or maybe love through gentle hands
that guide them on their way?

Do you think they dream of future times
when they would be king,
Or just enjoy their present life
while with their friends they sing?

Do they see acts of kindness
done for people who are poor?
Is the very best in everyone
what they are looking for?

And when the day is over
as they close their eyes to sleep,
Do they look forward to tomorrow
with its promises to keep?

If this is what the children see
then it should be no surprise
That the world would be a better place
if we all had children's eyes.

Tom Krause

Contributed By:

Tarla Dalal- is India's best-selling gastronomy expert, whose name has become synonymous with fine dining. Her books have been translated into Hindi, Gujarati, Marathi, Bengali, Dutch and Russian. She hosts a cookery show, *Cook it up with Tarla Dalal*. Her first book, *The Pleasures of Vegetarian Cooking*, is regarded as a classic in culinary literature.

જે ગમે જગત–ગુરુ દેવ જગદીશને 22

જે ગમે જગત–ગુરુ દેવ જગદીશને
તે તણો ખરખરો ફોક કરવો.
આપણો ચિંતવ્યો અર્થ કાંઈ નવ સરે
ઊગરે એક ઉદ્વેગ ધરવો.
હું કરું, હું કરું, એ જ અજ્ઞાનતા
શકટનો ભાર જેમ શ્વાન તાણે.
સૃષ્ટિ મંડાણ છે સર્વ એણી પેરે
જોગી જોગેશ્વરા કોકજાણે.
નીપજે નરથી તો કોઈ ના રહે દુખી
શત્રુ મારીને સૌ મિત્ર રાખે.
રાય ને રંક કોઈ દૃષ્ટે આવે નહીં
ભવન પર ભવન પર છત્ર દાખે.
ઋતુ લતા પત્ર ફળ ફૂલ આપે યથા
માનવી મૂર્ખ મન વ્યર્થ શોચે,
જેહના ભાગ્યમાં જે સમે જે લખ્યું
તેહને તે સમે તે જ પહોંચે.

ગ્રન્થ ગરબડ કરી વાત ન કરી ખરી
જેહને જે ગમે તેને પૂજે.
મન કર્મ વચનથી આપ માની લહે
સત્ય હો એ જ મન એમ સૂઝે.
સુખ સંસારી મિથ્યા કરી માનજો
કૃષ્ણ વિના બીજુ સર્વ કાચું.
જુગલ કર જોડી કરી
નરસૈંયો એમ કહે
જન્મ પ્રતિજન્મ હરિને જ જાચું

નરસિંહ મેહતા
ગુજરાત

Whatever Is Ordained By the Lord

No one should feel any remorse for any failure,
If it was so ordained and laid down by the Almighty

If one's planning and efforts do not result in success,
It only adds to one's miseries.

The ego enveloping any activity and the feeling that my creation is the sole cause of misery or remorse,
Is comparable to a dog under a moving cart feeling that he is pulling the frame

The creation of the cosmos is beyond the horizon of normal human belief;
Only a few saints and blessed beings can fathom its meaning.

If an individual could change the chain of events, then no one would remain unhappy;
One could then eradicate the enemy and sustain only friends-then no one would be rich or poor.
The illusion of life makes us scale the heights of abode after abode-like the sprouting of a variety of flowers and fruits in different seasons,
A foolish human being contemplates achieving this impossibility

Whatever has been therefore ordained by the Almighty,
Will be bestowed upon one at the appropriate time.

The preachings of the scriptures are sometimes confusing,
One should worship whoever one has faith in.

The ultimate goal, whether in thought, action or speech,
Is to have retaliation and be one with the spirit of truth.

The good things of life have to be renunciated in favour of the worship of Lord Krishna,
The other various desires are only a mirage.

With folded hands, the poet Narsinh prays to the Lord for His blessings,
In this life and for those to come.

Narsinh Mehta

Contributed By:

Sonal Mansingh - is a senior Odissi artiste and researcher. Initially she was trained in Bharat Natyam, and was inducted into the art of Odissi after meeting her husband.
With a degree in both Sanskrit and German, Sonal Mansingh is a follower of literature, poetry, language, sculpture and painting: 'Dance', she says, 'is a rare confluence of all these arts.' in 1977, this dancer, social activist and orator founded the Centre for Indian Classical Dances (CICD) in Delhi.

The Hound of Heaven 23

I fled Him, down the nights and down the days;
I fled Him, down the arches of the years;
I fled Him, down the labyrinthine ways
Of my own mind; and in the mist of tears
I hid from Him, and under running laughter.
Up vistaed hopes I sped;
And shot, precipitated,
Adown Titanic glooms of chasmed fears,
From those strong Feet that followed, followed after.
But with unhurrying chase,
And unperturbed pace,
Deliberate speed, majestic instancy,
They beat - and a Voice beat
More instant than the Feet -
'All things betray thee, who betrayest Me.'

I pleaded, outlaw-wise,
By many a hearted casement, curtained red,
Trellised with intertwining charities;
(For, though I knew His love who followed,
Yet was I sore adread
Lest, having Him, I must have naught beside).
But, if one little casement parted wide,
The gust of His approach would clash it to.
Fear wist not to evade, as Love wist to pursue.
Across the margent of the world I fled,
And troubled the gold gateways of the stars,
Smiting for shelter on their clanged bars;
Fretted to dulcet jars
And silvern chatter the pale ports o' the moon.
I said to Dawn: Be sudden-to Eve: Be soon;

With thy young skiey blossoms heap me over
From this tremendous Lover -
Float thy vague veil about me, lest He see!
I tempted all His servitors, but to find
My own betrayal in their constancy,
In faith to Him their fickleness to me,
Their traitorous trueness, and their loyal deceit.
To all swift things for swiftness did I sue;
Clung to the whistling mane of every wind.
But whether they swept, smoothly fleet,
The long savannahs of the blue;
Or whether, Thunder-driven,
They clanged his chariot 'thwart a heaven,
Plashy with flying lightnings round the spurn o' their feet:–
Fear wist not to evade as Love wist to pursue.
Still with unhurrying chase,
And unperturbed pace,
Deliberate speed, majestic instancy,
Came on the following Feet,
And a Voice above their beat
'Naught shelters thee, who wilt not shelter Me.'

I sought no more that after which I strayed
In face of man or maid;
But still within the little children's eyes
Seems something, something that replies,
They at least are for me, surely for me!
I turned me to them very wistfully;
But just as their young eyes grew sudden fair
With dawning answers there,
Their angel plucked them from me by the hair.
'Come then, ye other children, Nature's–share
Let me greet you lip to lip,
Let me twine with you caresses,

Wantoning
With our Lady-Mother's vagrant tresses,
Banqueting
With her in her wind-walled palace,
Underneath her azured dais,
Quaffing, as your taintless way is,
From a chalice
Lucent-weeping out of the dayspring.'
So it was done:
I in their delicate fellowship was one-
Drew the bolt of Nature's secrecies.
I knew all the swift importings
On the wilful face of skies;
I knew how the clouds arise
Spumed of the wild sea-snortings;
All that's born or dies
Rose and drooped with; made them shapers
Of mine own moods, or wailful or divine;
With them joyed and was bereaven.
I was heavy with the even,
When she lit her glimmering tapers
Round the day's dead sanctities.
I laughed in the morning's eyes.
I triumphed and I saddened with all weather,
Heaven and I wept together,
And its sweet tears were salt with mortal mine;
Against the red throb of its sunset-heart
I laid my own to beat,
And share commingling heat;
But not by that, by that, was eased my human smart.
In vain my tears were wet on Heaven's grey cheek.

For ah! we know not what each other says,
These things and I; in sound I speak

Their sound is but their stir, they speak by silences.
Nature, poor step dame, cannot slake my drouth;
Let her, if she would owe me,
Drop yon blue bosom-veil of sky, and show me
The breasts o' her tenderness;
Never did any milk of hers once bless
My thirsting mouth.
Nigh and nigh draws the chase,
With unperturbed pace,
Deliberate speed, majestic instancy;
And past those noised Feet
A voice comes yet more fleet
'Lo! naught contents thee, who content'st not Me!'

Naked I wait Thy love's uplifted stroke!
My harness piece by piece Thou hast hewn from me,
And smitten me to my knee;
I am defenceless utterly.
I slept, methinks, and woke,
And, slowly gazing, find me stripped in sleep.
In the rash lustihead of my young powers,
I shook the pillaring hours
And pulled my life upon me; grimed with smears,
I stand amid the dust o' the mounded years–
My mangled youth lies dead beneath the heap.
My days have crackled and gone up in smoke,
Have puffed and burst as sun-starts on a stream.
Yea, faileth now even dream
The dreamer, and the lute the lutanist;
Even the linked fantasies, in whose blossomy twist
I swung the earth a trinket at my wrist,

Are yielding; cords of all too weak account
For earth with heavy griefs so overplussed.

Ah! Is Thy love indeed
A weed, albeit an amaranthine weed,
Suffering no flowers except its own to mount?
Ah! must–
Designer infinite!–
Ah! must Thou char the wood ere Thou canst limn with it?
My freshness spent its wavering shower i' the dust;
And now my heart is a broken fount,
Wherein tear-drippings stagnate, spilt down ever
From the dank thoughts that shiver
Upon the sightful branches of my mind.
Such is; what is to be?
The pulp so bitter, how shall taste the rind?
I dimly guess what Time in mists confounds;
Yet ever and anon a trumpet sounds
From the hid battlements of Eternity;
Those shaken mists a space unsettle, then
Round the half-glimpsed turrets slowly wash again.
But not ere him who summoneth
I first have seen, enwound
With glooming robes purpureal, cypress-crowned;
His name I know, and what his trumpet saith.
Whether man's heart or life it be which yields
Thee harvest, must Thy harvest-fields
Be dunged with rotten death?
Now of that long pursuit
Comes on at hand the bruit;
That Voice is round me like a bursting sea:
'And is thy earth so marred,
Shattered in shard on shard?
Lo, all things fly thee, for thou fliest Me!
Strange, piteous, futile thing!
Wherefore should any set thee love apart?
Seeing none but I makes much of naught' (He said),

'And human love needs human meriting;
How hast thou merited–
Of all man's clotted clay the dingiest clot?
Alack, thou knowest not
How little worthy of any love thou art!
Whom wilt thou find to love ignoble thee,
Save Me, save only Me?
All which I took from thee I did but take,
Not for thy harms,
But just that thou might'st seek it in My arms.
All which thy child's mistake
Fancies as lost, I have stored for thee at home:
Rise, clasp My hand, and come!'
Halts by me that footfall;
Is my gloom, after all,
Shade of His hand, outstretched caressingly?
'Ah, fondest, blindest, weakest,
I am He whom thou seekest!
Thou dravest love from thee, who dravest Me.'

Francis Thompson

Contributed By:

Tarun Das - For decades, Tarun Das was the director general of the Confederation of Indian Industry (CII), India's leading industry association today. Mr Das has been on several boards including those of the Reserve Bank of India and Air India.

'You can't run away.'

From *Dies Slowly* 24

Slowly dies who doesn't turn the table upside down,
Who's unhappy at work,

Who doesn't risk the certainties for the unknown to pursue a dream,
Who doesn't allow himself to run away from wise suggestions,
At least once in a lifetime.

Slowly dies who doesn't travel, who doesn't read,
Who never listens to music, who doesn't find grace in himself,
Slowly dies who destroys his self-esteem,
Who spends every day to complain about either his bad luck or the never-ending rain.

Let's avoid death in small doses, keeping in mind that being alive always requests a much bigger effort than the simple fact of breathing.

Pablo Neruda

Contributed By:

Shobhaa Dé - has had a colourful spectrum of careers. She has been a fashion model, an editor, a copywriter, a journalist, a columnist and a novelist. She was the first editor of the magazines *Stardust* and *Society*, and has published seven extremely successful novels.

'It is simple, sincere, sensitive and stays with me at all times-especially when I'm searching for answers.'

The Love Song of J. Alfred Prufrock 25

Let us go then, you and I,
When the evening is spread out against the sky
Like a patient etherized upon a table;
Let us go, through certain half-deserted streets,
The muttering retreats
Of restless nights in one-night cheap hotels
And sawdust restaurants with oyster-shells:
Streets that follow like a tedious argument
Of insidious intent
To lead you to an overwhelming question . . .
Oh, do not ask, 'What is it?'
Let us go and make our visit.

In the room the women come and go
Talking of Michelangelo.

The yellow fog that rubs its back upon the window-panes,
The yellow smoke that rubs its muzzle on the window-panes
Licked its tongue into the corners of the evening,
Lingered upon the pools that stand in drains,
Let fall upon its back the soot that falls from chimneys,
Slipped by the terrace, made a sudden leap,
And seeing that it was a soft October night,
Curled once about the house, and fell asleep.

And indeed there will be time
For the yellow smoke that slides along the street,
Rubbing its back upon the window-panes;
There will be time, there will be time
To prepare a face to meet the faces that you meet;

There will be time to murder and create,
And time for all the works and days of hands
That lift and drop a question on your plate;
Time for you and time for me,
And time yet for a hundred indecisions,
And for a hundred visions and revisions,
Before the taking of a toast and tea.

In the room the women come and go
Talking of Michelangelo.

And indeed there will be time
To wonder, 'Do I dare?' and, 'Do I dare?'
Time to turn back and descend the stair,
With a bald spot in the middle of my hair--
[They will say: 'How his hair is growing thin!']
My morning coat, my collar mounting firmly to the chin,
My necktie rich and modest, but asserted by a simple pin--
[They will say: 'But how his arms and legs are thin!']
Do I dare
Disturb the universe?
In a minute there is time
For decisions and revisions which a minute will reverse.

For I have known them all already, known them all:--
Have known the evenings, mornings, afternoons,
I have measured out my life with coffee spoons;
I know the voices dying with a dying fall
Beneath the music from a farther room.
So how should I presume?

And I have known the eyes already, known them all--
The eyes that fix you in a formulated phrase,
And when I am formulated, sprawling on a pin,
When I am pinned and wriggling on the wall,

Then how should I begin
To spit out all the butt-ends of my days and ways?
And how should I presume?
And I have known the arms already, known them all–
Arms that are braceleted and white and bare
[But in the lamplight, downed with light brown hair!]
Is it perfume from a dress
That makes me so digress?
Arms that lie along a table, or wrap about a shawl.
And should I then presume?
And how should I begin?

Shall I say, I have gone at dusk through narrow streets
And watched the smoke that rises from the pipes
Of lonely men in shirt-sleeves, leaning out of windows?…

I should have been a pair of ragged claws
Scuttling across the floors of silent seas.

And the afternoon, the evening, sleeps so peacefully!
Smoothed by long fingers,
Asleep… tired… or it malingers,
Stretched on the floor, here beside you and me.
Should I, after tea and cakes and ices,

Have the strength to force the moment to its crisis?
But though I have wept and fasted, wept and prayed,
Though I have seen my head [grown slightly bald] brought in upon a platter,
I am no prophet–and here's no great matter;
I have seen the moment of my greatness flicker,
And I have seen the eternal Footman hold my coat, and snicker,
And in short, I was afraid.

And would it have been worth it, after all,
After the cups, the marmalade, the tea,

Among the porcelain, among some talk of you and me,
Would it have been worth while,
To have bitten off the matter with a smile,
To have squeezed the universe into a ball
To roll it toward some overwhelming question,
To say: 'I am Lazarus, come from the dead
Come back to tell you all, I shall tell you all'–
If one, settling a pillow by her head,
Should say: 'That is not what I meant at all.
That is not it, at all.'

And would it have been worth it, after all,
Would it have been worth while,
After the sunsets and the dooryards and the sprinkled streets,
After the novels, after the teacups, after the skirts that trail along the floor—
And this, and so much more?—
It is impossible to say just what I mean!
But as if a magic lantern threw the nerves in patterns on a screen:
Would it have been worth while
If one, settling a pillow or throwing off a shawl,
And turning toward the window, should say:
'That is not it at all,
That is not what I meant, at all.'

No! I am not Prince Hamlet, nor was meant to be;
Am an attendant lord, one that will do
To swell a progress, start a scene or two,
Advise the prince; no doubt, an easy tool,
Deferential, glad to be of use,
Politic, cautious, and meticulous;
Full of high sentence, but a bit obtuse
At times, indeed, almost ridiculous—
Almost, at times, the Fool.

I grow old… I grow old…
I shall wear the bottoms of my trousers rolled.
Shall I part my hair behind? Do I dare to eat a peach?
I shall wear white flannel trousers, and walk upon the beach.
I have heard the mermaids singing, each to each.

I do not think that they will sing to me.
I have seen them riding seaward on the waves
Combing the white hair of the waves blown back
When the wind blows the water white and black.

We have lingered in the chambers of the sea
By sea-girls wreathed with seaweed red and brown
Till human voices wake us, and we drown.

T. S. Eliot

Contributed By:

Professor Lord Meghnad Desai - is an economist and the author of over twenty books, including *Nehru's Hero: Dilip Kumar in the Life of India*. He is also director of the Centre for the Study of Global Governance at the London School of Economics. His research interests cover a wide spectrum and include inflation, unemployment, applied econometrics, financial innovation and Chinese economic reform.

'I regard this poem as the first modern poem in English, a reflection on life today. The language is beautiful, alas inimitable - a younger Desai failed to emulate in spite of many attempts.'

Anjolie Ela Menon - had already painted about forty canvases by the time she left high school. This artist, known for paintings that are infused with a 'feminine sensibility' and soulful eyes, worked and studied in Paris in the early sixties. A compulsive itinerant, her travels and her stint at the Atelier Fresque in the Ecole des Beaux Arts influenced her art. In addition to solo shows, and paintings in private and corporate collections, her works have been acquired by museums in India and abroad. Based in Delhi, she is also a well-known muralist, who has experimented with glass sculptures.

Alyque Padamsee - is a communications consultant. As an actor, he is internationally remembered for his role as Mohammed Ali Jinnah in Richard Attenborough's *Gandhi*. He was chief executive of Lintas India, a leading advertising agency for many years. As a stage director, he revolutionized Indian theatre with recreations of Broadway's *A Streetcar Named Desire* and *Joseph And the Amazing Technicolour Dreamcoat*. Recently, he directed an Indian rendition of *Romeo and Juliet*. He is now an advertising consultant and a social activist.

'Why do I respond to this poem? Because it speaks of everyday things but gives them poetic imagination. It's about nostalgia, love, growing old and death. Reading it for the 100th time, it still moves me.'

If no one listens to your call,
Walk alone.
If in fear they cower, mutely facing the wall,
O hapless one,
Open your mind and speak out alone.
If, as you cross the wilderness, they turn and desert you,
O hapless one,
Tread firmly on the thorns along the blood-lined track, and travel alone.
If, in the storm-troubled night, they dare not hold aloft the light,
O hapless one,
Ignite your own heart with the lightning and pain, and yourself become
The guiding light.

Rabindranath Tagore

(Translated from the Bengali by Indira Gandhi)

Contributed By:

Sonia Gandhi - is the president of India's century-old Congress party. Born in Ovassanio, Italy, she met her husband Rajiv Gandhi at Cambridge. Mr Gandhi was the third in line to be prime minister of independent India, and Sonia Gandhi subsequently became the third woman of foreign origin to be president of the Congress Party (after Nellie Gupta and Annie Besant). She was the chairperson of the ruling United Progressive Alliance in the Lok Sabha, until she resigned in March 2006.

'Rabindranath Tagore's "Walk Alone (Ekla Chalo Re)" never fails to move and inspire me. This poem was also a favourite with Indira Gandhi. Not satisfied with existing translations in English, she wrote her own. This poem is special because it is such an eloquent and passionate evocation of the virtue of courage - the courage to listen to one's inner voice, the courage to stand by one's convictions in the face of opposition, and the courage to unflinchingly face danger in defence of truth and justice.'

The Captain 27

Who can escape the sting of fate?
At best we can but feint and dodge,
We know someday the barb will lodge,
For some it's soon, for others late.
Though nature yields sometimes to reason
Not all transpires in timely season.

How dreadful - a slow sapping death
Where every moment's full of strife
And breathing's all that's left of life
And life, itself, not worth a breath.
We must accept the soul is leaving,
But nothing can arrest our grieving.

For solace, there still is the past
And grief is foiled by reveries -

The treasure of sweet memories
Of which, our hoard is rich and vast.
Each day we can produce a jewel
And grief is bound to lose the duel.

But why not gaze the other way
And build for him a monument,
Complete the work for which he spent
His each and every living day.
And thus the wounds of grief we suture
By looking at the past and future.

No one quite knows where he can be.

I have a vision-a quiet beach
He stands and gazes at the reach,
He boards a yacht, he's out at sea,
He navigates an endless ocean.
And I am lulled by this strange notion.

Nadir Godrej

Contributed By:

Nadir Godrej - is the managing director of Godrej Industries Ltd and director of numerous companies. He is active in research and has several patents to his credit. Mr Godrej has written a book of poems in English and French titled *Life & Other Poems.*

'In memory of my uncle, Naval Godrej (1916 - 1990), a good sailor and a great soul, I wrote it. I was very sad because my uncle was dying. I woke up in the night and suddenly the words appeared. We can't fight death but we mustn't let death win.'

Cosmic Murmur 28

In the din of city life
You cannot listen to the whispering murmur
of humanity

Come with me to the sobbing forest
where the trembling trees whisper
their soul-stirring tale.

For millions of years
these now tortured trees
have been swinging merrily
hand in hand

Shared life with birds and animals,
close companionship of colourful flora,
gleeful songs of
lakes and rivulets.

But now,
the craze for money of hardened man
chopping and slashing the tree's arms
have severed them from their life-long friends.

These wise old deities bemoan
the fast erosion of our human habitat,
not their personal plight.

With mutual co-operation
you can still save the universe.

Listen,
listen to their urgent call;
It's time.

Shiela Gujral

Contributed By:

I. K. Gujral - is a former prime minister of India. Mr Gujral served as India's foreign minister twice, and once as ambassador to Moscow. He served time in prison during World War II for his anti-British stance, whilst still managing to complete two doctorate degrees, including one in literature, at Lahore and New Delhi. An erstwhile member of Indira Gandhi's cabinet, he speaks fluent Urdu and spends his leisure creatively, writing Urdu couplets. He is also a former minister of external affairs in the Indian parliament.

Books 29

Books peek at me,
sad and wistful,
through the glass panes
of my book shelves.
These days
I don't meet them
for months on end.
The evenings I spent
in their company
now pass by
on the computer screen.
The books are restless;
they look lost
as if sleep-walking,
the human values
of cells that never die
that they taught me
are nowhere in sight.
The affinities they brought me
are all stripped bare
leaving only moist sighs.
You can hear them sob
when a page is turned.
Their pages have lost colour,
their words, meaning.
They now look like dead wood
which will no more
sprout meanings.
Phrases, sayings, maxims

are strewn across the pages
like discarded earthen cups
made redundant by glass tumblers.
There was a time
when turning the pages
would bring a strange taste to my tongue;
now the click of a finger
that opens up a whole world
is only a flitting blink.
All that is over now
the intimate contact with books.
One could lie down
with a book in one's chest,
or put it on one's lap,
take it in hand,
or place it on the knees
crossed into a book-stand.
They are not to be.
We used to read books
with a solemn bow,
and touched them reverently
with our foreheads.
Now, God willing,
knowledge will still
come to us,
but what about
the little pleasures
the books offered us
dried flowers and perfumed notes
between the pages;
contacts crafted through pretexts of borrowing,
or even,

dropping
or picking up a book?
perhaps,
they are never to be.

Gulzar

(Translated from the Urdu by J. P. Das.)

Contributed By:

Gulzar - A poet, lyricist, writer and director, Gulzar began his film career as an assistant to Bimal Roy. Gaining recognition as a sensitive lyricist, he turned his talents to conceptualising storylines and scripting. *Mere Apne* was the very first film he directed. Many more followed including the evergreen *Khamoshi*. Gulzar will forever be remembered for *Mirza Ghalib*, a television serial about the eponymous poet. He has also authored books on poetry, short stories and several books for children. Apart from numerous national awards such as the Lifetime Achievement Award and Filmfare trophies, he has also been conferred the prestigious Padma Bhushan.

'The poem explains it by itself. My passion for books, makes it my all time favourite, and so it has been with readers and listeners.'

A Strange Problem 30

I have a strange problem these days
The power to hate with all my heart
Is ebbing by the day

I want to hate the English
(They ruled us for two centuries)
But Shakespeare sidles up
To whom I owe so much

I want to hate the Muslims
But Ghalib stands before me
Tell me, is it possible to stand up
To him?

I want to hate the Sikhs
And Guru Nanak fills my vision
And my head is bowed

And this Kamban, this Thiagaraja, this
Muthuswamy…
A hundred thousand times I tell myself
They are not mine
They're from some place far South
But the heart does not rest
Till they are made mine

And that lover
Who betrayed me the first time
I'd as soon kill her as look at her!
I do see her, but

Sometimes she is a friend
Sometimes a mother
Often like a sister

And I drink from the cup of love, and still
All my days
I wander like a madman
In search of someone I can
Hate with all my heart
And ease it for a while
But precisely the opposite happens
Somewhere, sometime
I find someone
I cannot help but love

Day by day, this disease of love is growing
Rooted firmly in the fantasy
That one day my love
Will show me paradise

Kanwar Narain

(Translated from the Hindi by Pratik Kanjilal)

Contributed By:

Shekhar Gupta - Group CEO of the Indian Express Group of Publications and editor-in-chief of the *Indian Express*. A director of International Centre for Ethnic Studies, this senior journalist and columnist has also been senior editor at *India Today*. He masterminds the carefully orchestrated, unconventional show *Walk the Talk* for NDTV 24x7.

'It is a counter to the anger of the age and seems to speak from the Indian heart.'

Jana gana mana adhinayaka jaya he
Bharat bhagya vidhata
Punjab Sindh Gujarat Maratha
Dravida Utkala Banga
Vindhya Himachal Yamuna Ganga
Ucchala jaladhi taranga
Tubh shubha name jage
Tubh shubha ashisha mange
Gahe tubh jaya gatha
Jana gana mangaldayak jaya he
Bharat bhagya vidhata
Jaye he ! Jaye he ! Jaye he !
Jaye, jaye, jaye, jaye he

Rabindranath Tagore

Contributed By:

Anna Hazare - is a noted social worker. He is the winner of several felicitations, most notably the Padma Shri and the Padma Bhushan. He tirelessly fights against corruption and has made inspiring efforts to improve the living conditions of the poor, and promote societal ethics.

'The anthem inspires me to devote my life to the nation.'

Footprints in the Sand

One night I dreamed I was walking along the beach with the Lord.
Many scenes from my life flashed across the sky.
In each scene I noticed footprints in the sand.
Sometimes there were two sets of footprints,
other times there was only one.
This bothered me because I noticed that during the low periods of my life,
when I was suffering from anguish,
sorrow or defeat,
I could see only one set of footprints.
So I said to the Lord,
'You promised me Lord,
that if I followed you,
you would walk with me always.
But I have noticed that during the most trying periods of my life
there has only been one set of footprints in the sand.
Why, when I needed you most, have you not been there for me?'
The Lord replied,
'The times when you have seen only one set of footprints,
my child, is when I carried you.'

Mary Stevenson

Contributed By:

Dr Indira Hinduja - India's first test tube baby, Harsha, was the result of seminal research and the pioneering work of Dr Indira Hinduja. This has turned out to be a boon for infertile couples. Dr Hinduja is the only gynaecologist and obstetrician in India to have been awarded a post doctorate in the field of human In-vitro Fertilization (IVF) and Embryo Transfer from the Bombay University. She has been on the clinical faculty of the Seth G. S. Medical College and King Edward Memorial Hospital, Mumbai.

'Whenever I am at my lowest, these lines assure me that God is always there. This gives me the will power to look life in the eye and face any challenge, and to overcome all obstacles with a strong confidence because He is always with me.'

Jyotiraditya M. Scindia - was elected to the Lok Sabha in February 2002 from the constituency of Guna, formerly represented by his father, with a margin of victory more than 450,000, and is the crowned 'Maharaja' of Gwalior. He picked up managerial skills at Harvard and Stanford, and worked as an investment banker for Merrill Lynch and Morgan Stanley. He has also worked with the UN Economic Development Cell.

'This is not quite a poem but has given me tremendous faith in the past and present!'

From *Burnt Norton* 33

(No. 1 of 'Four Quartets)

Time present and time past
Are both perhaps present in time future,
And time future contained in time past.
If all time is eternally present
All time is unredeemable.
What might have been is an abstraction
Remaining a perpetual possibility
Only in a world of speculation.
What might have been and what has been
Point to one end, which is always present.
Footfalls echo in the memory
Down the passage which we did not take
Towards the door we never opened
Into the rose-garden. My words echo
Thus, in your mind.
But to what purpose
Disturbing the dust on a bowl of rose-leaves
I do not know.
Other echoes
Inhabit the garden. Shall we follow?
Quick, said the bird, find them, find them,
Round the corner. Through the first gate,
Into our first world, shall we follow
The deception of the thrush? Into our first world.
There they were, dignified, invisible,
Moving without pressure, over the dead leaves,
In the autumn heat, through the vibrant air,
And the bird called, in response to
The unheard music hidden in the shrubbery,
And the unseen eyebeam crossed, for the roses

Had the look of flowers that are looked at.
There they were as our guests, accepted and accepting.
So we moved, and they, in a formal pattern,
Along the empty alley, into the box circle,
To look down into the drained pool.
Dry the pool, dry concrete, brown edged,
And the pool was filled with water out of sunlight,
And the lotos rose, quietly, quietly,
The surface glittered out of heart of light,
And they were behind us, reflected in the pool.
Then a cloud passed, and the pool was empty.
Go, said the bird, for the leaves were full of children,
Hidden excitedly, containing laughter.
Go, go, go, said the bird: human kind
Cannot bear very much reality.
Time past and time future
What might have been and what has been
Point to one end, which is always present.

T. S. Eliot

Contributed By:

Prahlad Kakkar - is a maverick ad filmmaker who runs a diving school in Lakshwadeep, grows mangoes, sells tea and runs restaurants. A graduate from Fergusson College, Pune, he began his career in 1972 as an apprentice under Shyam Benegal. Later, he set up his own production house, Genesis. His distinctive, innovative commercials for Pepsi and Nestle are a guiding light to a generation of film-makers.

'The poem is very relevant in the context of children, who we cannot ignore in the present as they are the tomorrow, the future of the country. They must be nurtured like plants so that they grow into strong sturdy oaks that have strong roots.'

The National Prayer 34

The grand scene of the birth of Independent India:
In that mid-night, the flag of the ruler of two centuries lowered;
The tri-color fluttering at the Red Fort amidst National Anthem.
The first vision of Independent India dawned.

The rejoicing everywhere, happiness all around,
There was a tender cry: where is the Father of the Nation?
The white-clothed soul walking in the midst of sorrow and pain,
Injected by hatred and ego, the result of communal violence.

The father of the nation, Mahatma, walking barefoot
In the streets of Bengal for peace and harmony.
With the strength of blessed soul of the Mahatma
I pray to the Almighty: When will be the dawn of the second
vision?

Create thoughts in the minds of my people,
And transform those thoughts into action.
Embed the thought of Nation being bigger than
The individual, in the minds of leaders and people.

Help all the leaders of my country to give strength
And bless the nation with peace and prosperity.
Give strength to all my religious leaders to bring
Unity of Minds among all our billion people.

O Almighty, bless all my people to work and transform
Our country from a developing into a developed nation.
Let this second vision be born out of sweat of my people,
And bless our youth to live in a Developed India.

A. P. J. Abdul Kalam

Contributed By:

Dr A. P. J. Abdul Kalam - became the president of India on 25 July 2002. An eminent scientist and aeronautical engineer, he was the architect of India's missile development programme, and was responsible for the development of the AGNI and PRITHVI missiles. Importantly, he made a significant contribution as project director of India's first indigenous satellite launch vehicle, which was put into orbit in July 1980. Dr Kalam was the principal scientific advisor to the government of India as a cabinet minister, from 1999-2001. A recipient of the Padma Bhushan and the Bharat Ratna, he has also written a number of books, including *Wings of Fire* and *India 2020 - A Vision for the New Millennium*, a road map for transforming the country.

I met a traveller from an antique land
Who said:- 'Two vast and trunkless legs of stone
Stand in the desert. Near them, on the sand,
Half sunk, a shattered visage lies, whose frown,
And wrinkled lip and sneer of cold command,
Tell that its sculptor well those passions read
Which yet survive, stamped on these lifeless things,
The hand that mocked them, and the heart that fed;
And on the pedestal these words appear:
'My name is Ozymandias, King of Kings:
Look on my works, ye Mighty, and despair!'
Nothing beside remains. Round the decay
Of that colossal wreck, boundless and bare
The lone and level sands stretch far away.'

Percy Bysshe Shelley

Contributed By:

K. V. Kamath - is the MD & CEO of ICICI. Under his leadership, ICICI achieved the status of being the first Indian company to be listed on the New York stock exchange. He has served on government committees to formulate infrastructure and shipping policy. He is also a member of the governing board of various educational institutions.

'The poem talks about the perils of arrogance and the risk of impermanence of a person's achievements - and teaches the virtue of humility.'

Abraham Lincoln's Letter to His Son's Teacher 36

He will have to learn, I know,
that all men are not just,
all men are not true.
But teach him also that
for every scoundrel there is a hero;
that for every selfish politician,
there is a dedicated leader...
Teach him for every enemy there is a friend,
Teach him to learn to lose ...
and also to enjoy winning.
It will take time, I know;
but teach him if you can,
that a dollar earned is of far more value
than five found...
Steer him away from envy,
if you can,
teach him the secret of
quiet laughter.
Let him learn early that
the bullies are the easiest to lick...
Teach him, if you can,
the wonder of books...
But also give him quiet time
to ponder the eternal mystery of birds in the sky,
bees in the sun,
and the flowers on a green hillside.
In the school teach him
it is far honourable to fail
than to cheat...
Teach him to have faith

in his own ideas,
even if everyone tells him
they are wrong...
Teach him to be gentle
with gentle people,
and tough with the tough.
Try to give my son
the strength not to follow the crowd
when everyone is getting on the band wagon...
Teach him to listen to all men...
but teach him also to filter
all he hears on a screen of truth,
and take only the good
that comes through.
Teach him if you can,
how to laugh when he is sad...
Teach him there is no shame in tears,
Teach him to scoff at cynics
and to beware of too much sweetness...
Teach him to sell his brawn
and brain to the highest bidders
but never to put a price-tag
on his heart and soul.
Teach him to close his ears
to a howling mob
and to stand and fight
if he thinks he's right.
Treat him gently,
but do not cuddle him,
because only the test
of fire makes fine steel.
Let him have the courage
to be impatient...

let him have the patience to be brave.
Teach him always
to have sublime faith in himself,
because then he will have
sublime faith in mankind.
This is a big order,
but see what you can do...
He is such a fine little fellow,
my son!

Abraham Lincoln

Contributed By:

Shah Rukh Khan - is a household name and a celluloid phenomenon. After his debut in the TV serial *Fauji*, Khan's acting career unfolded with an unprecedented singularity. Perhaps humility was his virtue, but it has sustained him with undiminished vigour. Shah Rukh Khan has acted in dozens of box office successes including *Deewana* opposite the late Divya Bharati, *Kal Ho Na Ho, Kabhi Khushi Khabhi Gham, Dev, Mohabbatein, Main Hoon Na* and *Kabhi Alvida na Kehna*.

'This is my favourite poem because my father gave it to me to read when I was fourteen. It believes in competition and compassion, traits I have grown to believe are the essence of a good life.'

Discourse from Srimad Bhagawad Gita

19. Therefore, always perform actions which should be done, without attachment;
For, by performing action without attachment, man attains the Supreme.

25. As the ignorant act from attachment to action, O Bharata,
So should the wise act without attachment, wishing the welfare of the world.

35. Better one's own Dharma though devoid of merit,
Than the Dharma of another, well discharged.
Better is death in one's own Dharma;
The Dharma of another is fraught with danger.

Contributed By:

Faqir Kohli - Born in Peshawar, Faqir Kohli is known as the father of Indian information technology. After graduating from Punjab University, Lahore, and Queen's University in Canada with a degree in Electrical Engineering, he proceeded to the MIT. Earlier a power engineer, Mr Kohli built Tata Consultancy Services, in the face of widespread scepticism, into a globally recognised software services giant. Along the way, he inspired a generation of technocrats to write the Indian IT success story.

'The stanzas above (taken from the Chinmaya Mission's translation) capture, for me, the essence of Karma Yoga. I believe that India and Indians have a great future. These ancient verses promise us happiness and progress if each of us fulfils our Dharma (loosely, duty and destiny) without selfish cause and without envy of others.'

For as long as space endures, and for as long as all living beings remain, until then may I too abide, to dispel the misery of the world.

Master Shantideva

Contributed By:

His Holiness the Dalai Lama - His Holiness the 14th Dalai Lama Tenzin Gyatso, is the Tibetan Buddhist spiritual leader and exiled head of state of the Tibetan people. He was born to a peasant family as Lhamo Dhondrub in 1935, in Taktser, a small village in northeastern Tibet. He was recognized at the age of two, in accordance with Tibetan tradition, as the reincarnation of his predecessor, the 13th Dalai Lama. Enthroned in 1950 at the tender age of fifteen, the Dalai Lama has since been an inspiration to admirers around the world. In 1989, he received the Nobel Peace Prize. Tibetans normally refer to His Holiness as Yeshe Norbu, the wish-fulfilling gem or simply Kundun - The Presence.

'The verse from the eight-century Buddhist master Shantideva's "Guide to the Bodhisattva's Way of Life" has been one of the most inspiring prayers for me.'

Sonnet 16

But wherefore do not you a mightier way
Make war upon this bloody tyrant, Time?
And fortify yourself in your decay
With means more blessed than my barren rhyme?
Now stand you on the top of happy hours,
And many maiden gardens yet unset
With virtuous wish would bear your living flowers,
Much liker than your painted counterfeit:
So should the lines of life that life repair,
Which this, Time's pencil, or my pupil pen,
Neither in inward worth nor outward fair,
Can make you live yourself in eyes of men.
To give away yourself keeps yourself still,
And you must live, drawn by your own sweet skill.

William Shakespeare

Contributed By:

Amartya Sen

Morning Express **40**

ALONG the wind-swept platform, pinched and white,
The travellers stand in pools of wintry light,
Offering themselves to morn's long, slanting arrows.
The train's due; porters trundle laden barrows.
The train steams in, volleying resplendent clouds
Of sun-blown vapour. Hither and about,
Scared people hurry, storming the doors in crowds.
The officials seem to waken with a shout,
Resolved to hoist and plunder; some to the vans
Leap; others rumble the milk in gleaming cans.
Boys, indolent-eyed, from baskets leaning back,
Question each face; a man with a hammer steals
Stooping from coach to coach; with clang and clack
Touches and tests, and listens to the wheels.
Guard sounds a warning whistle, points to the clock
With brandished flag, and on his folded flock
Claps the last door: the monster grunts: 'Enough!'
Tightening his load of links with pant and puff.
Under the arch, then forth into blue day,
Glide the processional windows on their way,
And glimpse the stately folk who sit at ease
To view the world like kings taking the seas
in prosperous weather: drifting banners tell
Their progress to the counties; with them goes
The clamour of their journeying; while those
Who sped them stand to wave a last farewell

Siegfried Sassoon

Contributed By:

Amartya Sen – is the preeminent social economist of our times. He has graced institutions such as Trinity College in Cambridge University, the London School of Economics, Oxford University and, most recently, Harvard University where he teaches as one of eighteen elite professors that report directly to the university's president. Born in Shantiniketan, Bengal and educated at the Presidency College, Calcutta, he is a professor of economics and philosophy, specializing in areas of welfare economics such as poverty, famine and collective choice.

His publications, seminal in their insistence on asking questions of value, serve to influence the priorities of economists and development workers; and the policies of the United Nations. They include, *Collective Choice and Social Welfare* (1970); *Development as Freedom* (1999); *Rationality and Freedom* (2002) and *The Argumentative Indian* (2005). A fellow of the British Academy, a former president of the Econometric Society, the American Economic Association, the Indian Economic Association and the International Economic Association, his accolades most famously include the Bharat Ratna and the Nobel Prize for Economics (1998).

'Most of my favourite poems are in Bengali, but I won't try them in English metamorphosis, since poetry loses its spirit in translation. The sonnet of Shakespeare chosen here is an all-time favourite of mine, but it can keep one awake at night (the human predicament has rarely been captured as well anywhere else), and seems quite unsuitable for a book dedicated to helping children. Hence the second poem, from Siegfried Sassoon, which is a cheerful morning thought, and favourite enough to be included here, if only to affirm that the world has robust frivolity as well as tragedy and grim resolution.'

Silent, the Lord of the world
Eyes from the heavenly height,
Girt by his far-shining train.
Us, who with banners unfurl'd,
Fight life's many-chanc'd fight
Madly below, in pain.

Then saith the Lord to his own :-
'See ye the battle below?
Turmoil of death and of birth!
Too long let we them groan.
Haste, arise ye, and go;
Carry my peace upon the earth.'

Gladly they rise at his call;
Gladly they take his command;
Gladly descend to the plain.
Alas! How few of them all
Those willing servants shall stand
In their Master's presence again!
Some in the tumult are lost;
Baffled, bewilder'd, they stray.
Some as prisoners draw breath.
Others, –the bravest are cross'd,
On the height of their bold-follow'd way,
By the swift rushing missile of Death.
Hardly, hardly shall one
Come, with countenance bright,
O'er the cloud wrapt, perilous plain:
His Master's errand well done,
Safe through the smoke of the fight,
Back to his Master again.

Contributed By:

Anand Mahindra - is the managing director and vice chairman of Mahindra & Mahindra Ltd. He is also the co-promoter of Kotak Mahindra Finance Ltd, one of India's most prominent finance companies. He writes frequently on business and general economic subjects in India's leading business magazines.

'The poem is at once fatalistic and inspirational. It speaks of how few of us sent down to the world and to life, are able to fulfill our entrusted mission of fighting for peace on earth - and that's fatalistic. Yet, what is inspiring is that it reflects a belief in "free will", and in the opportunity that a higher power gives us to create our own destinies and make a genuine difference to our own lives, and the lives of others.'

ऐसे हैं सुख सपन हमारे 42

ऐसे हैं सुख सपन हमारे
बन बन कर मिट जाते जैसे, बालू के घर नदी किनारे ॥

लहरें आती बह जातीं
रेखाएँ बस रह रह जातीं
जाती लहरें कह कह जाती, जाते पल को कौन पुकारे ।

ऐसी इन सपनों की माया
जल पर जैसे चाँद की छाया
चाँद किसी के हाथ न आया, चाहे जितने हाथ पसारे ।

मन भर आया नैना छलकें
गालों पर दो आँसू ढलके
याद किये क्यों सपने कल के, बीते को तू क्यों न बिसारे ।

स्व. पं. नरेंद्र शर्मा

Dreams of Happiness

Such are our dreams of happiness
Like sand castles on riverbanks

The waves wash the shores
leave behind just lines in the sand
And murmur as they depart
Why call out to time passed?

Such is the illusion of dreams
Like the image of the moon on water
No one can quite touch the moon, try as they might.

The heart grows heavy, the eyes overflow
Teardrops roll down the cheeks
Why hold on the dreams of yesterday, why not let the past be?

Pandit Narendra Sharma

Contributed By:

Lata Mangeshkar - Hailed as India's nightingale, Lata Mangeshkar has been active in all spheres of Indian music, from ghazals and bhajans to Indian pop and film songs. A Phalke award winner for her contribution to Indian music and cinema, Lata Mangeshkar was recently honoured with India's highest civilian award, the Bharat Ratna. In 1991, the Guinness Book of World Records acclaimed her as the most recorded artiste in the world with over 30,000 recordings in twenty Indian languages. The numbers today would be way beyond that!

Say Not the Struggle Naught Availeth 43

Say not the struggle naught availeth,
The labour and the wounds are vain,
The enemy faints not, nor faileth,
And as things have been they remain;

If hopes were dupes, fears may be liars;
It may be, in yon smoke conceal'd,
Your comrades chase e'en now the fliers,
And, but for you, possess the field.

For while the tired waves vainly breaking
Seems here no painful inch to gain,
Far back, through creeks and inlets making,
Comes silent, flooding in, the main.

And not by eastern windows only,
When daylight comes, comes in the light,
In front, the sun climbs slow, how slowly!
But westward, look, the land is bright!

Arthur Hugh Clough

Contributed By:

Justice Sujata Manohar - Educated at Oxford, and Lincoln's Inn, London, Sujata Vasant Manohar has had a brilliant academic and professional career. She was the first woman to be elevated as a judge on the bench of the Bombay High Court. In 1999, she was also the first woman chief justice of the Bombay High Court. One of five women judges selected to constitute a tribunal for recording evidence and giving findings at the World Women's Congress for a

Healthy Planet (1991), held at Miami, Mrs Manohar was signatory to the Declaration of Miami. Significantly, she was chairperson of the committee of judges established by the Bombay High Court to set up family courts in Maharashtra. Passionate about individual liberty and a known humanitarian, this former justice of the Supreme Court is a member of the National Human Rights Commission of India.

'I like it not so much for its poetic qualities as for its optimism and message of hope.'

क्रांतीचा - जयजयकार 44

(अन्नत्याग करून मृत्यूच्या दारात पाऊल टाकताना राजबंद्यांच्या ओठावर असलेच गाणे स्फुरले नसेल काय ?)

गर्जा जयजयकार क्रांतिचा गर्जा जयजयकार
अन् वज्रांचे छातीवरती घ्या झेलून प्रहार !
खळखळुद्या या अदय शृंखला हातापायांत
पोलादाची काय तमा मरणाच्या दारात ?
सर्पांनो उद्दाम, आवळा कसूनिया पाश
पिचेल मनगट परी उरातिल अभंग आवेश
तडिताघाते कोसळेल का तारांचा संभार
कधीही तारांचा संभार
गर्जा जयजयकार क्रांतिचा गर्जा जयजयकार !

क्रुद्ध भूक पोटात घालुद्या खुशाल थैमान
कुरतडुद्या आतडी करूद्या रक्ताचे पान
संहारक काली, तुज देती बळीच आव्हान
बलशाली मरणाहुन आहे अमुचा अभिमान
मृत्युंजय आम्ही ! आम्हाला कसले कारागार ?
अहो हे कसले कारागार ?
गर्जा जयजयकार क्रांतिचा गर्जा जयजयकार !

पदोपदी पसरुन निखारे आपुल्याच हाती
होउनिया बेहोष धावलो ध्येयपथावरती
कधि न थांबलो विश्रांतीस्तव, पाहिले न मागे
बांधु न शकले प्रीतीचे वा कीर्तीचे धागे
एकच तारा समोर आणिक पायतळी अंगार
होता पायतळी अंगार
गर्जा जयजयकार क्रांतिचा गर्जा जयजयकार !

श्वासांनो, जा वायूसंगे ओलांडुनि भिंत
अन् आईला कळवा अमुच्या हृदयातील खंत
सांगा वेडी तुझी मुले ही या अंधारात
बद्ध करांनी अखेरचा तुज करिती प्रणिपात
तुझ्या मुक्तिचे एकच होते वेड परी अनिवार
तयांना वेड परी अनिवार
गर्जा जयजयकार क्रांतिचा गर्जा जयजयकार !

नाचविता ध्वज तुझा गुंतले शृंखलेत हात
तुझ्या यशाचे पवाड गाता गळ्यात ये तात
चरणांचे तव पूजन केले म्हणुनि गुन्हेगार
देता जीवन-अर्घ्य तुला ठरलो वेडेपीर
देशिल ना पण तुझ्या कुशीचा वेड्यांना आधार
आई, वेड्यांना आधार
गर्जा जयजयकार क्रांतिचा गर्जा जयजयकार ।

कशास आई, भिजविसि डोळे, उजळ तुझे भाल
रात्रीच्या गर्भात उद्याचा असे उष: काल
सरणावरती आज आमुची पेटताच प्रेते
उठतिल त्या ज्वाळांतून भावी क्रांतिचे नेते
लोहदण्ड तव पायांमधले खळाखळा तुटणार
आई, खळाखळा तुटणार
गर्जा जयजयकार क्रांतिचा गर्जा जयजयकार !

आता कर ओंकारा, तांडव गिळावया घास
नाचत गर्जत टाक बळींच्या गळ्यावरी फास
रक्तमांस लुटण्यास गिधाडे येउ देत क्रूर
पहा मोकळे केले आता त्यासाठी ऊर
शरिरांचा कर सुखेनैव या सुखेनैव संहार
मरणा, सुखेनैव संहार
गर्जा जयजयकार क्रांतिचा गर्जा जयजयकार !

कुसुमाग्रज

Victory, Victory of Revolution

(*A group on hunger strike, facing death, sang this inspiring song to sustain their protest*)

Roar victory, victory of revolution. Roar victory, victory,
Tolerate the hammering chest–endure the diamond-hard blows
Let the iron chains jangle on your wrists and ankles
We are at the door of death. What do we care
About our steely troubles?
Inspiration from the hymns grips us
As a snake encircles his prey like a rope.
A mountain of woes has befallen us
The star filled sky has fallen on us.

Even then, echo victory, victory.
To revolution, Victory, victory.

Do the revolutionary dance even if
The fire of hunger rages in your belly.
Let your guts be drawn by hunger,
Demanding blood.
At the time of sacrifice
The attacker's deeds are meaningless; we are prepared to do without.
We are more proud than the power of death.
We await the end–how could we be afraid of prison?

Echo Victory! Victorious revolution!
Let's roar! Victory! Victorious!

Burning coals are spread on our path.
With every step we take, these cannot burn our soles.

We accept this. We are non-violent marchers.
We run along, without a care for burning coals
We die, not stop, on our way to enact our slogan.
Kali, you who demand sacrifice, we accept your challenge
Our pride is greater than the power of death.
Do not stop to rest
Brothers, we are tied by the strings of love
Of fame, of duty.
The star of victory shines before us and beneath our burning feet
Our steps burn.

Roar: Victory! Victorious revolution!
Roar: Victory! victorious!

Our breaths move on the wind
Cross the wall of obstruction.
Tell our mothers of the pain in our hearts
Tell them their sons moves in darkness.
The marchers salute you with a smile–the last greeting
Our only ambition is the salvation of victory
This is our compulsive insanity.

Roar: Victory! Victorious revolution!
Roar: Victory! victorious!

As we dance with the flag
Your wrists may become entangled in chains.
O father, as we sing our song of victory
The garland of success will be around your neck.
We have said the prayer. Now we have been declared criminals.
Bless us so we may live our motto in life
Though they call us mad.
Hold us up
That is the support we insane people need.

Roar: Victory! Victorious revolution!
Roar: Victory! victorious!

Dear mother, why are you eyes wet again and again?
Hold your head high, radiant with pride
After the darkness of night, we will see the dawn.
When our bodies are burned on the banks of the river
The revolutionary face will rise once more from the flames
The chains will fall. The jangling will end.
The rattling will end.

Roar: Victory! Victorious revolution!
Roar: Victory! victorious!

Now perform Aumkar, the Tandav dance
Drop the chains as you dance
Destroy the vultures that feed on our flesh
Let your body sway to the rhythm of joy and freedom
You will enjoy the sight.

Roar: Victory! Victorious revolution!
Roar: Victory! Victorious!

Kusumagraj

Contributed By:

Medha Patkar - The eco-crusader has been a central organiser and strategist of the Narmada Bachao Andolan (NBA), a people's movement organized to stop the construction of a series of dams planned for the Narmada river. In 1985, Patkar began mobilising massive marches and rallies against the project, and, although the protests were peaceful, she was repeatedly beaten and arrested by the police. She almost died during a twenty-two day hunger strike in 1991. Undaunted, she undertook two more long protest fasts in 1993 and 1994. Patkar has helped establish a network of activists across the country - the National Alliance of People's Movements. Her actions lead to an unprecedented independent review of the dam project by the World Bank.

கல்வி 45

கற்க கசடறக் கற்பவை;
கற்றபின் நிற்க அதற்குத் தக.

திருவள்ளுவர்

Education

Learn well all that is to be learnt;
Thereafter let your conduct be worthy of that learning.

Tiruvalluvar

Contributed By:

Cho Ramaswami - Member of Parliament and editor of the Tamil weekly, *Thuglak*, has multiple careers. He is an actor, commentator, journalist, and now television personality. An inimitable satirist, he is also a member of the Rajya Sabha.

'These are couplets (over 1000 in number) providing education, moral values and guidelines for human existence.'

Celebrating 46

The sun rises and celebrates
The sky embraces and celebrates
Winds blow and celebrate
Rivers flow and celebrate
Birds sing and celebrate
Peacocks dance and celebrate
Trees flower and celebrate
Buds blossom and celebrate
We smile and serve
Meditate and celebrate

Sri Sri Ravi Shankar

Contributed By:

Sri Sri Ravi Shankar - Born in Bangalore, India, Sri Sri Ravi Shankar became a scholar of vedic literature at a young age. He established the Art of Living Foundation in 1982 to promote self-development and health-related educational programs, through the Sudarshan Kriya technique, his own creation. In more recent times, he served on the advisory board of Yale University's School of Divinity and chaired the International Conference of Religions at Kyoto, Japan. In 1995, Sri Sri Ravi Shankar spoke at the United Nations' 50th Anniversary celebration and in 2000, he addressed the UN's Millennium World Peace Summit of Religious and Spiritual Leaders.

The World's Need 47

So many gods, so many creeds,
So many paths that wind and wind,
While just the art of being kind
Is all the sad world needs.

Ella Wheeler Wilcox

Contributed By:

Julio Ribeiro - can be described as the grand old man of the Indian police. He has earned accolades as police commissioner of Mumbai, director general of the Central Reserve Police, director general of the police of Gujarat and, of course, as the much decorated director general of the police of Punjab during its worst years of terrorism. The 'Super Cop' was subsequently ambassador to Romania. A recipient of the Padma Bhushan award, Ribeiro has had a ringside view of crime and violence. The 'Mohalla Committees' he spearheaded are designed to promote communal cooperation in Mumbai.

'I could not remember who wrote this poem, but the words have been etched in my memory since I was a boy.'

Sonnet for Jehangir 48

These landscapes have the colour of absence.
Endless departures have been made from them,
Are being made, will in future be made.
These landscapes are endlessly departing
From ours to a time beyond ours, to arrive
Without luggage or passports, but themselves,
Tranquil, demanding no favours,
Bringing their own suns, their own weather.

Remote suns, changing weather,
Odours of impending darkness, wingbeats
Heard on the canvas. What is flying there?
Will a great bird descend to tear and rend?
Amnesties hang in the air and no answers
Save the sounds of the colours of absence.

Dom Moraes

Contributed By:

Jehangir Sabavala - is an eminent artist. Apart from solo shows, he has participated in several international auctions. He was awarded the Padma Shri in 1977.

'Out of no conceit, even though the poem is dedicated to me... but, out of admiration for the writer of beautiful poetry, the well known Indo-Anglian poet, Dom Moraes. His verses, always so felicitously phrased and magically nuanced, have in this poem, so perceptively articulated the concerns of my "paintings" of that period.'

Under One Small Star 49

My apologies to chance for calling it necessity.
My apologies to necessity if I'm mistaken, after all.
Please, don't be angry, happiness, that I take you as my due.
May my dead be patient with the way my memories fade.
My apologies to time for all the world I overlook each second.
My apologies to past loves for thinking that the latest is the first.
Forgive me, distant wars, for bringing flowers home.
Forgive me, open wounds, for pricking my finger.
I apologize for my record of minuets to those who cry from the depths.
I apologize to those who wait in railway stations for being asleep today at five a.m.
Pardon me, hounded hope, for laughing from time to time.
Pardon me, deserts, that I don't rush to you bearing a spoonful of water.
And you, falcon, unchanging year after year, always in the same cage,
your gaze always fixed on the same point in space,
forgive me, even if it turns out you were stuffed.
My apologies to the felled tree for the table's four legs.
My apologies to great questions for small answers.
Truth, please don't pay me much attention.
Dignity, please be magnanimous.
Bear with me, O mystery of existence, as I pluck the occasional thread from your train.
Soul, don't take offense that I've only got you now and then.
My apologies to everything that I can't be everywhere at once.
My apologies to everyone that I can't be each woman and each man.

I know I won't be justified as long as I live,
Since I myself stand in my own way.
Don't bear me ill will, speech, that I borrow weighty words,
then labor heavily so that they may seem light.

Wislawa Szymborska

Contributed By:

Leela Samson - is a Bharat Natyam dancer, hailed as one of India's most brilliant performers, who combines geometrical precision with vibrancy. She is an outstanding representative of Kalakshetra, the famous institute for the classical arts founded by the late Rukmini Devi on the Chennai coast. A distinguished soloist and choreographer, Leela is also a writer on dance, and is noted for her book *Rhythm in Joy* (1987). She is a recipient of the Padma Shri and Sangeet Natak Akademi awards. Ms Samson is based in Delhi, where she teaches and directs her own dance company, Spanda, which is a Sanskrit term for 'pulse'.

'Because it captures life and all that we miss, in the blur of living it.'

And Still I Rise 50

You may write me down in history
With your bitter, twisted lies,
You may trod me in the very dirt
But still, like dust, I'll rise.

Does my sassiness upset you?
Why are you beset with gloom?
'Cause I walk like I've got oil wells
Pumping in my living room.

Just like moons and like suns,
With the certainty of tides,
Just like hopes springing high,
Still I'll rise.

Did you want to see me broken?
Bowed head and lowered eyes?
Shoulders falling down like teardrops.
Weakened by my soulful cries.

Does my haughtiness offend you?
Don't you take it awful hard
'Cause I laugh like I've got gold mines
Diggin' in my own back yard.

You may shoot me with your words,
You may cut me with your eyes,
You may kill me with your hatefulness,
But still, like air, I'll rise.

Does my sexiness upset you?
Does it come as a surprise
That I dance like I've got diamonds
At the meeting of my thighs?

Out of the huts of history's shame
I rise
Up from a past that's rooted in pain
I rise
I'm a black ocean, leaping and wide,
Welling and swelling I bear in the tide.
Leaving behind nights of terror and fear
I rise
Into a daybreak that's wondrously clear
I rise
Bringing the gifts that my ancestors gave,
I am the dream and the hope of the slave.
I rise
I rise
I rise.

Maya Angelou

Contributed By:

Malavika Sangghvi - Described as 'a chronicler of social mores' by the *New York Times*, Malavika Sangghvi has had a successful career as a journalist, editor, poet and television host. In the late 80's, she was the India editor of *Harpers & Queens*, UK, and frequently broadcasted on the BBC. Her weekly column that ran in *Mid-Day* for fifteen years is widely discussed, and she recently published a book commissioned by the Indian Merchant's Chamber on India's women. Literary accomplishments aside, Ms Sangghvi has hosted her own chat show, *Bombay Times*, on Star TV. She currently lives in Mumbai and is a consulting editor at the Times Group.

If I should die, think only this of me:
That there's some corner of a foreign field
That is forever England. There shall be
In that rich earth a richer dust concealed;
A dust whom England bore, shaped, made aware,
Gave, once, her flowers to love, her ways to roam;
A body of England's, breathing English air,
Washed by the rivers, blest by suns of home.

And think, this heart, all evil shed away,
A pulse in the eternal mind, no less
Gives somewhere back the thoughts by England given;
Her sights and sounds; dreams happy as her day;
And laughter, learnt of friends; and gentleness,
In hearts at peace, under an English heaven.

Rupert Brooke

Contributed By:

Rajdeep Sardesai - is the feisty and spirited host, political commentator and editor of New Delhi Television (NDTV). A cricket enthusiast, he studied Economics and Sociology in Mumbai and Oxford, after which he worked as a cub reporter. Before his foray into television, he was city editor and head-news service, *Times of India*, Bombay.

'It's a poem that I read in school for the first time, and have returned to periodically since. It's a poem that captures the grief, and the spirit of an ordinary citizen and patriot.'

The Second Coming 52

Turning and turning in the widening gyre
The falcon cannot hear the falconer;
Things fall apart; the centre cannot hold;
The blood-dimmed tide is loosed, and everywhere
The ceremony of innocence is drowned;
The best lack all convictions while the worst
Are full of passionate intensity.

Surely some revelation is at hand;
Surely the Second Coming is at hand.
The Second Coming! Hardly are those words out
When a vast image out of Spiritus Mundi
Troubles my sight; somewhere in the sands of the desert
A shape with lion body and the head of a man,
A gaze blank and pitiless as the sun,
Is moving its slow thighs, while all about it
Reel shadows of the indignant desert birds.
The darkness drops again; but now I know
That twenty centuries of stony sleep
Were vexed to nightmare by a rocking cradle,
And what rough beast, its hour come round at last,
Slouches toward Bethlehem to be born?

W. B. Yeats

Contributed By:

Aparna Sen - Actress, screenwriter and director, Aparna Sen has been a celebrated member of the Indian cinema for four decades. She made her directorial debut with an award winning English film *36 Chowringhee Lane*, which she also scripted. Daughter of the renowned film historian, critic, and film-maker, Chidananda Dasgupta, her directorial work also includes memorable films such as *Sati, Parama, Yugant*, and more latterly, *Mr and Mrs Iyer*. She has served on many juries at film festivals in India and overseas. She was conferred the Padma Shri and is also the recipient of the Satyajit Ray Lifetime Achievement Award.

'*It is difficult to specify why a poem is one's favourite! Indeed, it is rarely the same poem that remains a favourite at all times... more often, different poems occupy one's thoughts at different phases of one's life or during different moods...*

Still, The Second Coming is one of the poems that I continue to read most often and one which always seems to be relevant to the times! Most so now, while the world is in the grip of violence-"the centre cannot hold/ Mere anarchy is loosed upon the world..."

And, in our country, while fundamentalist forces raise their ugly heads everywhere and while human life becomes the most expendable commodity, we watch in silent despair

"...and everywhere/ The ceremony of innocence is drowned/The best–lack all conviction, while the worst/Are full of passionate intensity."

My favourite lines—ones that give me goose bumps—are "And what rough beast, its hour come round at last,/Slouches towards Bethlehem to be born?" Is the coming prophet then a beast without mercy?'

आज अगर खामोश रहे तो ... 53

आज अगर खामोश रहे तो
कल सन्नाटा छायेगा ।
हर बस्ती में आग लगेगी
हर घर जल जायेगा ।
और उस सन्नाटे से फिर
एक सदा ये आयेगी ।
कोई नहीं है, कोई नहीं है
कोई नहीं है, कोई नहीं ।

साहिर लुधियानवी

If We Keep Silent Today . . .

If we keep silent today
Our tomorrow will fall still
Every village will burst into flames
Every house will burn
And from that stillness will arise
This echo,
Nobody here, there is nobody here
There is nobody here, nobody

Saahir Ludhianvi

Contributed By:

Teesta Setalvad - Originally a journalist, she is a human rights activist and co-editor of *Communalism Combat*, the only Indian magazine entirely focused on ending communalism. Mrs Setalvad is the director of KHOJ, a project which promotes secular education in schools and is the secretary of Citizens for Justice and Peace. Recently she was the convener of the Concerned Citizens Tribunal that investigated the killings in Gujarat. She has received several national and international human rights awards, including the Nuremberg International Human Rights Award, the Pax Christi International Peace Award, the PUCL Human Rights Journalism Award and the Dalit Liberation Education Trust's Human Rights Award.

The Exequy 54

ACCEPT, thou shrine of my dead saint,
Instead of dirges, this complaint;
And for sweet flowers to crown thy hearse
Receive a strew of weeping verse
From thy grieved friend, whom thou might'st see
Quite melted into tears for thee.

Dear loss! since thy untimely fate,
My task hath been to meditate
On thee, on thee; thou art the book,
The library whereon I look,
Though almost blind. For thee, loved clay,
I languish out, not live, the day . . .
Using no other exercise
But what I practice with mine eyes
By which wet glasses I find out
How lazily time creeps about
To one that mourns: this, only this,
My exercise and business is.
So I compute the weary hours
With signs dissolved into showers

Nor wonder if my time to thus
Backward and most preposterous

Thou hast benighted me; thy set
This eve of blackness did beget,
Who wast my day (tho' overcast
Before thou hadst thy noon-tide past):
And I remember must in tears,
Thou scarce hadst seen so many years
As day tells hours. By thy clear sun
My love and fortune first did run;

But thou wilt never more appear
Folded within my hemisphere,
Since both thy light and motion,
Like a fled star, is fall'n and gone;
And 'twixt me and my soul's dear wish
An earth now interposed is,
Which such a strange eclipse doth make
As ne'er was read in almanac

I could allow thee for a time
To darken me and my sad clime;
Were it a month, a year, or ten,
I would thy exile live till then,
And all that space my mirth adjourn,
So thou wouldst promise to return,
And putting off thy ashy shroud,
At length disperse this sorrow's cloud.

But woe is me! the longest date
Too narrow is to calculate
These empty hopes: never shall I
Be so much blest as to descry
A glimpse of thee, till that day come
Which shall the earth to cinders doom,
And a fierce fever must calcine
The body of this world like thine,
My little world. That fit of fire
Once off, our bodies shall aspire
To our souls' bliss: then we shall rise
And view ourselves with clearer eyes
In that calm region where no night
Can hide us from each other's sight.

Meantime thou hast her, earth; much good
May my harm do thee. Since it stood
With heaven's will I might not call
Her longer mine, I give thee all

My short-lived right and interest
In her whom living I loved best.
With a most free and bounteous grief
I give thee what I could not keep
Be kind to her, and prithee look
Thou write into thy doomsday book
Each parcel of this rarity
Which in thy casket shrined doth lie.
See that thou make thy reckoning straight
And yield her back again by weight
For thou must audit on thy trust
Each grain and atom of this dust
As thou wilt answer Him that lent,
Not gave thee, my dear monument.
So close the ground, and 'bout her shade
Black curtains draw, my bride is laid.

Sleep on, my Love, in thy cold bed
Never to be disquieted!
My last good-night! Thou wilt not wake
Till I thy fate shall overtake:
Till age, or grief, or sickness must
Marry my body to that dust
It so much loves, and fill the room
My heart keeps empty in thy tomb.
Stay for me there, I will not fail
To meet thee in that hollow vale.
And think not much of my delay:
I am already on the way,
And follow thee with all the speed
Desire can make, or sorrows breed.
Each minute is a short degree
And ev'ry hour a step towards thee.
At night when I betake to rest
Next morn I rise nearer my west
Of life, almost by eight hours' sail,
Than we sleep breathed his drowsy gale.

Thus from the sun my bottom steers,
And my day's compass downward bears;
Nor labor I stem the tide
Through which to thee I swiftly glide.

'Tis true, with shame and grief I yield,
Thou, like the van, first tookst the field;
And gotten hast the victory
In thus adventuring to die
Before me, whose more years might crave
A just precedence in the grave.
But hark! my pulse, like a soft drum
Beats my approach, tells thee I come;
And slow howe'er my marches be,
I shall at last sit down by thee.

The thought of this bids me go on,
And wait my dissolution
With hope and comfort. Dear, forgive
The crime, I am content to live
Divided, with but half a heart,
Till we shall meet and never part.

Henry King
Bishop of Chichester

Contributed By:

Vikram Seth - A literary genius, Vikram Seth is an internationally renowned novelist and poet now living in the UK. Educated in India, and at Oxford, Stanford and Nanking Universities, he is the author of several globally acclaimed books including *A Suitable Boy, An Equal Music* and, most recently, *Two Lives*. Mr Seth always had a passion for poetry and literature; in fact, he cut short his Ph. D in order to pursue writing. His first book, *The Golden Gate*, was written in 1986 and was dubbed 'Byronesque' by critics due to its 690 tetrameter sonnets. He also left his mark on the stage, when the English National Opera commissioned him to write a libretto based on the Greek myth of Arion and the Dolphin.

The Pied Piper of Hamelin 55

I.

Hamelin town's in Brunswick,
By famous Hanover city;
The river Weser, deep and wide,
Washes its wall on the southern side;
A pleasanter spot you never spied;
But, when begins my ditty,
Almost five hundred years ago,
To see the townsfolk suffer so
From vermin, was a pity.

II.

Rats!
They fought the dogs and killed the cats,
And bit the babies in the cradles,
And ate the cheeses out of the vats,
And licked the soup from the cooks' own ladles,
Split open the kegs of salted sprats,
Made nests inside men's Sunday hats,
And even spoiled the women's chats,
By drowning their speaking
With shrieking and squeaking
In fifty different sharps and flats.

III.

At last the people in a body
To the Town Hall came flocking:
''Tis clear,' cried they, 'our Mayor's a noddy;
And as for our Corporation–shocking
To think we buy gowns lined with ermine

For dolts that can't or won't determine
What's best to rid us of our vermin
You hope, because you're old and obese,
To find in the furry civic robe ease?
Rouse up, sirs! Give your brains a racking
To find the remedy we're lacking,
Or, sure as fate, we'll send you packing!'
At this the Mayor and Corporation
Quaked with a mighty consternation.

IV.
An hour they sate in council,
At length the Mayor broke silence:
'For a guilder I'd my ermine gown sell;
I wish I were a mile hence!
It's easy to bid one rack one's brain-
I'm sure my poor head aches again
I've scratched it so, and all in vain.
Oh for a trap, a trap, a trap!'
Just as he said this, what should hap
At the chamber door but a gentle tap?
'Bless us,' cried the Mayor, 'what's that?'
(With the Corporation as he sat,
Looking little though wondrous fat;
Nor brighter was his eye, nor moister
Than a too-long-opened oyster,
Save when at noon his paunch grew mutinous
For a plate of turtle green and glutinous)
'Only a scraping of shoes on the mat
Anything like the sound of a rat
Makes my heart go pit-a-pat!'

V.
'Come in!' the Mayor cried, looking bigger:
And in did come the strangest figure!
His queer long coat from heel to head
Was half of yellow and half of red,
And he himself was tall and thin,
With sharp blue eyes, each like a pin,
And light loose hair, yet swarthy skin,
No tuft on cheek nor beard on chin,
But lips where smiles went out and in;
There was no guessing his kith and kin!
And nobody could enough admire
The tall man and his quaint attire.
Quoth one: 'It's as my great-grandsire,
Starting up at the Trump of Doom's tone,
Had walked this way from his painted tombstone!'

VI.
He advanced to the council table:
And, 'Please your honours,' said he, 'I'm able,
By means of a secret charm, to draw
All creatures living beneath the sun,
That creep or swim or fly or run,
After me so as you never saw!
And I chiefly use my charm
On creatures that do people harm,
The mole and toad and newt and viper;
And people call me the Pied Piper.'
(And here they noticed round his neck
A scarf of red and yellow stripe,
To match with his coat of the selfsame check;
And at the scarf's end hung a pipe;
And his fingers, they noticed, were ever straying

As if impatient to be playing
Upon this pipe, as low it dangled
Over his vesture so old-fangled.)
'Yet,' said he, 'poor piper as I am,
In Tartary I freed the Cham,
Last June, from his huge swarms of gnats;
I eased in Asia the Nizam
Of a monstrous brood of vampire-bats:
And, as for what your brain bewilders,
If I can rid your town of rats
Will you give me a thousand guilders?'
'One? Fifty thousand!' was the exclamation
Of the astonished Mayor and Corporation.

VII.
Into the street the Piper stepped,
Smiling first a little smile,
As if he knew what magic slept
In his quiet pipe the while;
Then, like a musical adept,
To blow the pipe his lips he wrinkled,
And green and blue his sharp eyes twinkled,
Like a candle flame where salt is sprinkled;
And ere three shrill notes the pipe uttered,
You heard as if an army muttered;
And the muttering grew to a grumbling;
And the grumbling grew to a mighty rumbling;
And out of the houses the rats came tumbling.
Great rats, small rats, lean rats, brawny rats,
Brown rats, black rats, grey rats, tawny rats,
Grave old plodders, gay young friskers,
Fathers, mothers, uncles, cousins,
Cocking tails and pricking whiskers,

Families by tens and dozens,
Brothers, sisters, husbands, wives–
Followed the Piper for their lives.
From street to street he piped advancing,
And step for step they followed dancing,
Until they came to the river Weser,
Wherein all plunged and perished!
-Save one who, stout as Julius Caesar,
Swam across and lived to carry
(As he, the manuscript he cherished)
To Rat-land home his commentary:
Which was, 'At the first shrill notes of the pipe
I heard a sound as of scraping tripe,
And putting apples, wondrous ripe,
Into a cider-press's gripe:
And a moving away of pickle-tub-boards,
And a leaving ajar of conserve-cupboards,
And a drawing the corks of train-oil-flasks,
And a breaking the hoops of butter-casks:
And it seemed as if a voice
(Sweeter far than by harp or by psaltery
Is breathed) called out "Oh, rats, rejoice!
The world is grown to one vast drysaltery!
So munch on, crunch on, take your nuncheon,
Breakfast, supper, dinner, luncheon!"
And just as a bulky sugar-puncheon,
All ready staved, like a great sun shone
Glorious scarce an inch before me,
Just as methought it said "Come, bore me!"
-I found the Weser rolling o'er me.'

VIII.
You should have heard the Hamelin people

Ringing the bells till they rocked the steeple.
'Go,' cried the Mayor, 'and get long poles!
Poke out the nests and block up the holes!
Consult with carpenters and builders,
And leave in our town not even a trace
Of the rats!' when suddenly, up the face
Of the Piper perked in the market-place,
With a, 'First, if you please, my thousand guilders!'

IX.

A thousand guilders! The Mayor looked blue;
So did the Corporation too.
For council dinners made rare havoc
With Claret, Moselle, Vin-deGrave, Hock;
And half the money would replenish
The cellar's biggest butt with Rhenish
To pay this sum to a wandering fellow
With a gypsy coat of red and yellow!
'Beside,' quoth the Mayor with a knowing wink,
'Our business was done at the river's brink;
We saw with our eyes the vermin sink,
And what's dead can't come to life, I think.
So, friend, we're not the folks to shrink
From the duty of giving you something for drink,
And a matter of money to put in your poke;
But, as for the guilders, what we spoke
Of them, as you very well know, was in joke.
Beside, our losses have made us thrifty.
A thousand guilders! Come, take fifty!'

X.

The Piper's face fell, and he cried
'No trifling! I can't wait. Beside,

I’ve promised to visit by dinner-time
Bagdad, and accept the prime
Of the Head Cook's pottage, all he's rich in,
For having left, in the Caliph's kitchen,
Of a nest of scorpions no survivor:
With him I proved no bargain-driver,
With you, don't think I'll bate a stiver!
And folks who put me in a passion
May find me pipe to another fashion.’

XI.

‘How?’ cried the Mayor, ‘d’ye think I brook
Being worse treated than a Cook?
Insulted by a lazy ribald
With idle pipe and vesture piebald?
You threaten us, fellow? Do your worst,
Blow your pipe there till you burst!’

XII.

Once more he stepped into the street
And to his lips again
Laid his long pipe of smooth straight cane;
And ere he blew three notes (such sweet
Soft notes as yet musician's cunning
Never gave the enraptured air)
There was a rustling, that seemed like a bustling
Of merry crowds justling at pitching and hustling,
Small feet were pattering, wooden shoes clattering,
Little hands clapping and little tongues chattering,
And, like fowls in a farmyard when barley is scattering,
Out came the children running.
All the little boys and girls,
With rosy cheeks and flaxen curls,

And sparkling eyes and teeth like pearls,
Tripping and skipping, ran merrily after
The wonderful music with shouting and laughter.

XIII.

The Mayor was dumb, and the Council stood
As if they were changed into blocks of wood,
Unable to move a step, or cry
To the children merrily skipping by,
Could only follow with the eye
That joyous crowd at the Piper's back.
But how the Mayor was on the rack,
And the wretched Council's bosoms beat,
As the Piper turned from the High Street
To where the Weser rolled its waters
Right in the way of their sons and daughters!
However he turned from South to West,
And to Koppelberg Hill his steps addressed,
And after him the children pressed;
Great was the joy in every breast.
'He never can cross that mighty top!
He's forced to let the piping drop,
And we shall see our children stop!'
When, lo, as they reached the mountain's side,
A wondrous portal opened wide,
As if a cavern was suddenly hollowed;
And the Piper advanced and the children followed,
And when all were in to the very last,
The door in the mountainside shut fast.
Did I say, all? No! One was lame,
And could not dance the whole of the way;
And in after years, if you would blame
His sadness, he was used to say,–

'It's dull in our town since my playmates left!
I can't forget that I'm bereft
Of all the pleasant sights they see,
Which the Piper also promised me.
For he led us, he said, to a joyous land,
Joining the town and just at hand,
Where waters gushed and fruit-trees grew,
And flowers put forth a fairer hue,
And everything was strange and new;
The sparrows were brighter than peacocks here,
And their dogs outran our fallow deer,
And honey-bees had lost their stings,
And horses were born with eagles' wings:
And just as I became assured
My lame foot would be speedily cured,
The music stopped and I stood still,
And found myself outside the Hill,
Left alone against my will,
To go now limping as before,
And never hear of that country more!'

XIV.

Alas, alas for Hamelin!
There came into many a burgher's pate
A text which says, that heaven's Gate
Opes to the rich at as easy rate
As the needle's eye takes a camel in!
The Mayor sent East, West, North, and South,
To offer the Piper, by word of mouth,
Wherever it was men's lot to find him,
Silver and gold to his heart's content,
If he'd only return the way he went,
And bring the children behind him.

But when they saw 'twas a lost endeavour,
And Piper and dancers were gone for ever,
They made a decree that lawyers never
Should think their records dated duly
If, after the day of the month and year,
These words did not as well appear,
'And so long after what happened here
On the Twenty-second of July,
Thirteen hundred and seventy-six:'
And the better in memory to fix
The place of the children's last retreat,
They called it, the Pied Piper's Street.
Where any one playing on pipe or tabor
Was sure for the future to lose his labour.
Nor suffered they hostelry or tavern
To shock with mirth a street so solemn;
But opposite the place of the cavern
They wrote the story on a column,
And on the great church-window painted
The same, to make the world acquainted
How their children were stolen away;
And there it stands to this very day.
And I must not omit to say
That in Transylvania there's a tribe
Of alien people that ascribe
The outlandish ways and dress
On which their neighbours lay such stress,
To their fathers and mothers having risen
Out of some subterraneous prison
Into which they were trepanned
Long time ago in a mighty band
Out of Hamelin town in Brunswick land,
But how or why, they don't understand.

XV.

So, Willy, let you and me be wipers
Of scores out with all men–especially pipers!
And, whether they pipe us free from rats or from mice,
If we've promised them aught, let us keep our promise!

Robert Browning

Contributed By:

Naseeruddin Shah - The multi-talented actor is indeed in the league of extraordinary gentlemen. He is also an integral part of theatre, having directed and acted in several Hindi and English plays. He has won critical acclaim in India and internationally.

'It is the first poem I ever memorised (as a punishment) and realised its amazingly lucid imagery. It's the most "reciteable" poem. The words are like music. It had something to do with my becoming an actor.'

অন্তর মম বিকশিত করো 56

অন্তর মম বিকশিত করো
অন্তরতর হে ।
নির্মল করো, উজ্জ্বল করো,
সুন্দর করো হে ।
জাগ্রত করো, উদ্যত করো,
নির্ভয় করো হে ।
মঙ্গল করো, নিরলস নিঃসংশয় করো হে ।
অন্তর মম বিকশিত করো,
অন্তরতর হে ।

যুক্ত করো হে সবার সঙ্গে,
মুক্ত করো হে বন্ধ,
সঞ্চার করো সকল কর্মে
শান্ত তোমার ছন্দ ।
চরণপদ্মে মম চিত নিঃস্পন্দিত করো হে,
নন্দিত করো, নন্দিত করো,
নন্দিত করো হে ।
অন্তর মম বিকশিত করো
অন্তরতর হে ।

রবীন্দ্রনাথ ঠাকুর

Contributed By:

Pandit Ravi Shankar - is a legendary sitarist and composer. In the 1960's, he collaborated with Ustad Ali Akbar Khan and Ustad Alla Rakha to introduce Indian music to the west. He has also successfully collaborated with the likes of George Harrison, Yehudi Menuhin and Phillip Glasse. He has composed extensively for films and ballets in India, Canada, Europe and the United States. It is no surprise therefore, that he is the recipient of several awards and honours including fourteen doctorates, the Padma Vibhushan, Desikottam, the Magsaysay award, two Grammys and the Fukuoka Grand Prize which was bestowed on him by Japan. In 1986 he was nominated as a member of the Rajya Sabha.

Closing the Gap 57

Closing the gap to your streaming hair my arms
Stretch across the white lightning-hit air.
Through split trees, spit-ripped rivers,
Old ghosts come crashing,
Bearing the bones of poems.

Flights of geese fan out from your delta,
Point to the spice islands and lakes of gold
That travelers sketch in their treacherous lore.
But my ship knows the one course it must take
To reach your foreshore, rest its unicorn prow.

I beach. The sweat pricks up like rust in my pores.
South of the boomeranged future, your trail dries.
The spade offers its testimony:
A memory of desert agaves
That knocks at childhood's door

With the sharpened shafts of shadows.

Ranjit Hoskote

Contributed By:

Laxman Shreshtha - is an eminent artist. The renowned painter left his aristocratic home in Nepal to pursue his passion. Having lived in Paris after his student days at the JJ College of Art, he now lives in Mumbai.

'I find it visually complex and studded with mysteries when the partially clear one is directly facing insight.'

The Ballad of Father Gilligan 58

The old priest Peter Gilligan
Was weary night and day;
For half his flock were in their beds,
Or under green sods lay.

Once while he nodded on a chair,
At the moth-hour of eve,
Another poor man sent for him,
And he began to grieve.

'I have not rest, nor joy, nor peace,
For people die and die';
And after cried he, 'God forgive!
My body spake, not I!'

He knelt, and leaning on the chair
He prayed and fell asleep;
And the moth-hour went from the fields;
And stars began to peep.

They slowly into millions grew,
And leaves shook in the wind,
And God covered the world with shade,
And whispered to mankind.

Upon the time of a sparrow-chirp
When the moths came once more,
The old priest Peter Gilligan
Stood upright on the floor.

'Mavrone, mavrone! the man has died,
while I slept on the chair.'
He roused his horse of its sleep,
And rode with little care.
He rode now as he never rode,
By rocky lane and fen;
The sick man's wife opened the door:
'Father! you come again!'

'And is the poor man dead?' he cried.
'He died an hour ago.'
The old priest, Peter Gilligan,
In grief swayed to and fro.

'When you were gone, he turned and died
As merry as a bird.'
The old priest, Peter Gilligan,
He knelt him at that word.

'He Who hath made the night of stars
For souls who tire and bleed,
Sent one of His great angels down
To help me in my need.

'He Who is wrapped in purple robes,
With planets in His care,
Had pity on the least of things
Asleep upon a chair.'

W. B. Yeats

Contributed By:

Pesi Shroff - is an ace jockey. He is also the vice-president of the Jockeys Association of India and has raced many winning horses successfully past the finishing line at the derby to be a bankable veteran in the field.

हर गुमाँ है एतबार 59

हर गुमाँ है एतबार
शुक्रिया परवरदीगार
हाय ये कैसी बहार
बाग़बाँ है अश्कबार
मैं ओ मेरा ज़प्ते-ग़म
तू ओ तेरा कारोबार

इक अरसे के बाद भी अब तक ताज़ा तेरी बातें हैं
शाम वही है सहर वही है और वो ही बरसातें हैं

हर आहट पर यूँ लगता है जैसे तेरा आना हो
लेकिन कड़वा सच कहता है ये सब झूठी बातें हैं

जगजीत सिंह

Belief

Every fault, in you we trust
Thank you, O dear Lord

O how cruel the spring
That saddens even gardeners

Me and the emotions that I cannot express
You and your world that goes on none the less

Time has not erased your words
The evenings are the same, the mornings and so are the rains

Every footfall heralds your possible arrival
But bitter truth says that all these words are just lies

Jagjit Singh

Contributed By:

Jagjit Singh - is one of India's most eminent ghazal singers. Trained under the honorable Ustad Jamal Khan, he received early recognition for his talent by HMV and EMI India. Mr Singh, whose performances are heard regularly at film and television releases, has created a new interest in ghazal poetry, receiving accolades from the music industry and state governments in recognition of his talent. Apart from his own riyaaz and performances, he mentors young musicians and involves himself in charitable organisations such as CRY and ALMA.

Who 60

In the blue of the sky, in the green of the forest,
Whose is the hand that has painted the glow?
When the winds were asleep in the womb of the ether,
Who was it that roused them and bade them to blow?

He is lost in the heart, in the cavern of Nature,
He is found in the brain where He builds up the thought:
In the pattern and bloom of the flowers He is woven,
In the luminous net of the stars He is caught.

In the strength of a man, in the beauty of woman,
In the laugh of a boy, in the blush of a girl;
The hand that sent Jupiter spinning through heaven,
Spends all its cunning to fashion a curl.

There are His works and His veils and His shadows;
But where is He then? by what name is He known?
Is He Brahma or Vishnu? a man or a woman?
Bodied or bodiless? twin or alone?

We have love for a boy who is dark and resplendent,
A woman is our Lord, naked and fierce.
We have seen Him a-muse on the snow of the mountains,
We have watched Him at work in the heart of the spheres.

We will tell the whole world of His ways and His cunning;
He has the rapture of torture and passion and pain;
He delights in our sorrow and drives us to weeping,
Then lures with His joy and His beauty again.

All music is only the sound of His laughter,
All beauty the smile of His passionate bliss;
Our lives are His heart-beats, our rapture the bridal
Of Radha and Krishna, our love is their kiss.

He is strength that is loud in the blare of the trumpets,
And He rides in the car and He strikes in the spears;
He slays without stint and is full of compassion;
He wars for the world and its ultimate years.

In the sweep of the worlds, in the surge of the ages,
Ineffable, mighty, majestic and pure,
Beyond the last pinnacle seized by the thinker
He is throned in His seats that forever endure.

The Master of man and his infinite Lover,
He is close to our hearts, had we vision to see;
We are blind with our pride and the pomp of our passions,
We are bound in our thoughts where we hold ourselves free.

It is He in the sun who is ageless and deathless,
And into the midnight His shadow is thrown;
When darkness was blind and engulfed within darkness,
He was seated within it immense and alone.

Sri Aurobindo

Contributed By:

Dr Karan Singh - is a political scientist, philosopher, environmentalist, educationist and a former cabinet minister. Most importantly, he was the head of the state of Jammu and Kashmir for eighteen years, first as regent, then as elected sadar-i-riyasat, and finally as governor. Dr Singh was on Indira Gandhi's cabinet as minister for tourism and civil aviation; was minister for health and family planning, education and culture, and the Indian ambassador to the USA. A former member of the Rajya Sabha, he has composed and recited devotional songs in his mother tongue, Dogri, and is a connoisseur of Indian classical music.

ओ निस्संग ममेतर 61

आज फिर एक बार
मैं प्यार को जगाता हूँ
खोल सब मुँदे द्वार
इस अगुरु-धूम-गन्ध-रुँधे सोने के घर के
हर कोने को
सुनहली खुली धूप में निल्हाता हूँ।
तुम जो मेरी हो, मुझ में हो,
सघनतम निविड में
मैं ही जो हो अनन्य
तुम्हें मैं दूर बाहर से, प्रान्तर से,
देशावर से, कालेतर से
तल से, अतल से, धरा से, सागर से,
अन्तरीक्ष से,
निर्व्यास तेजस् के निर्गभीर शून्य आकर से
मैं, समाहित, अन्तःपूत,
मन्त्राहूत कर तुम्हें
ओ निस्संग ममेतर
ओ अभिन्न प्यार,
ओ धनी,
आज फिर एक बार
तुम को बुलाता हूँ -
और जो मैं हूँ, जो जाना-पहचाना,
जिया-अपनाया है, मेरा है,
धन है, संचय है, उस की एक-एक कली को
न्यौछावर लुटाता हूँ।
२
जिन शिखरों की
हेम-मज्जित उँगलियों ने
निर्विकल्प इंगित से
जिस निर्व्यास उजाले को

मेरे स्तब्ध मानस में गीत की लहर -सा
छाया है तुम्हारा स्वर ।
और रसास्वाद : मेरी स्मृति अभिभूत है ।
मैंने तुम्हें छुआ है
मेरी मुट्ठियों में भरी हुई तुम
मेरी उँगलियों बीच छन कर बही हो -
कण प्रतिकण आप्त, स्पृष्ट, भुक्त ।
मैंने तुम्हें चूमा है
और हर चुम्बन की तप्त, लाल, अयस्कठोर छाप
मेरा हर रक्त-कण धारे है ।

आह ! पर मैंने तुम्हें जाना नहीं ।

५
नहीं ! मैंने तुम्हें केवल मात्र जाना है ।
देखा नहीं मैंने कभी,
सुना नहीं, छुआ नहीं,
किया नहीं रसास्वाद-
ओ स्वतःप्रमाण ! मैंने
तुम्हें जाना,
केवल मात्र जाना है ।

देख मैं सका नहीं :
दीठ रही ओछी, क्योंकि तुम समग्र एक विश्व हो
छू सका नहीं :
अधूरा रहा स्पर्श क्योंकि तुम तरल हो, वायवी हो
पहचान सका नहीं : तुम
मायाविनि, कामरूपा हो ।

किन्तु, हाँ, पकड़ सका -
पकड़ सका, भोग सका
क्योंकि जीवनानुभूति
बिजली-सी त्वरग, अमोघ एक पंजा है

बलिष्ठ;
एक जाल निर्वारणीय :
अनुभूति से तो
कभी, कहीं, कुछ नहीं
बच के निकलता !

६
जीवनानुभूति : एक पंजा कि जिस में
तुम्हारे साथ मैं भी तो पकड़ में
आ गया हूँ !
एक जाल, जिस में
तुम्हारे साथ मैं भी बँध गया हूँ।
जीवनानुभूति :
एक चक्की । एक कोल्हू ।
समय की अजस्र धार का घुमाया हुआ
पर्वती घराट् एक अविराम ।
एक भट्ठी, एक आवाँ स्वत:तप्त :
अनुभूति !

७
तुम्हें केवल मात्र जाना है,
केवल मात्र तुम्हें जाना है,
तुम्हें जाना है, अप्रमाद तुम्हें जपा है,
तुम्हें स्मरा है ।
और मैंने देखा है
और मेरी स्मृति ने
मेरी देखी सारी रूप-राशि को इकाई दी है ।
मैंने सुना है --
और मेरी अविकल्प स्मृति ने
सभी स्वर एक मूर्छना में गूँथ डाले हैं ।
-- सूँघा, और स्मृति ने
विकीर्ण सब गन्धों को
चयित कर दिया एक वृन्त में एक ही वसन्त के ।

-- मैंने छुआ है :
और मेरे ज्ञान ने असंख्य माया-मूर्त्तियों को
दी है वह संहति अचूक
जो-मात्र मेरी पहचानी है
जिसे-मात्र मैंने चाहा है ।
-- मैंने चूमा है,
और, ओ आस्वाद्य मेरी !
ले गयी है प्रत्यभिज्ञा मुझे उस उत्स तक
जिस की पीयूषवर्षी, अनवद्य, अद्वितीय धार
मुझे आप्यायित करती है ।

हाँ, मैंने तुम्हें जाना है, मैं जानता हूँ,
पहचानता हूँ, सांगोपांग;
और भूलता नहीं हूँ -- कभी भूल नहीं सकता !

भूलता नहीं हूँ
कभी भूल नहीं सकता
और मैं बिखरना नहीं चाहता ।
आज, मन्त्राहूत ओ प्रियस्व मेरी !

मुझ को जो कहना है, वह इस धधकते क्षण में --
बाग्देवता की यज्ञ-ज्वाला जब तक अभी
जलती है मेरी इस आविष्ट जिह्वा पर,
तब तक -- मैं कह लूँ :
मेरे ही दाह का हुताशन हो साक्षी मेरा !

८

ओ आहूत !
ओ प्रत्यक्ष !
अप्रतिम !
ओ स्वयंप्रतिष्ठ !
सुनो संकल्प मेरा :

मैंने छुआ है, और मैं छुआ गया हूँ;
मैंने चूमा है, और मैं चूमा गया हूँ;
मैं विजेता हूँ, और मुझे जीत लिया गया है;
मैं हूँ, और मैं दे दिया गया हूँ;
मैं जिया हूँ, और मेरे भीतर से जो लिया गया है
मैं मिटा हूँ, मैं पराभूत हूँ, मैं तिरोहित हूँ,
मैं अवतरित हुआ हूँ, मैं आत्मसात् हूँ,
अमर्त्य, कालजित् हूँ ।

मैं चला हूँ
पहचानकर,
प्रकाश में,
दिक्-प्रबुद्ध,
लक्ष्यसिद्ध ।
इसी बल
जहाँ-जहाँ पहचान हुई, मैंने
वह ठाँव छोड़ दी;
ममता ने तरिणी को तीर-ओर मोड़ा-
वह डोर मैंने तोड़ दी ।
हर लीक पोंछी, हर डगर मिटा दी, हर दीप
निवा मैंने
बढ़ अन्धकार में
अपनी धमनी
तेरे साथ जोड़ दी ।

९
ओ मेरी सह-तितीर्षु,
हमीं तो सागर हैं
जिस के हम किनारे हैं क्योंकि जिसे हमने
पार कर लिया है ।

ओ मेरी सहयायिनि,
हमीं वह निर्मल तल-दर्शी वापी हैं

जिसे हम ओक -भर पीते हैं --
बार-बार, तृषा से, तृप्ति से, आमोद से, कौतुक से,
क्योंकि हमीं छिपा वह उत्स हैं जो उसे
पूरित किये रहता है ।

ओ मेरी सहधर्मा,
छू दे यह मेरा कर : आहुति दे दूँ --
हमीं याजक हैं, हमीं यज्ञ,
जिस में हुत हमीं परस्परेष्टि ।

ओ मेरी अतृप्त, दु:शम्य धधक, मेरी होता,
ओ मेरी हविष्यान्न,
आ तू, मुझे खा
जैसे मैंने तुझे खाया है
प्रसादवत् ।
हम परस्पराशी हैं क्योंकि परस्परपोषी हैं,
परस्परजीवी हैं ।

१०
ओ सहजन्मा, सह-सुभगा
नित्योढ़ा,
सहभोक्ता,
सहजीवा, कल्याणी ।

११
ओ मेरे पुण्य-प्रभव,
मेरे आलोक-स्नात, पद्म-पत्रस्थ जल-बिन्दु,
मेरी आँखों के तारे,
को ध्रुव, ओ चंचल,
को तपोजात,
मेरे कोटि-कोटि लहरों से मँजे एकमात्र मोती
को विश्व-प्रतिम,
अब तू इस कृती सीप को अपने में समेट ले,

यह परिदृश्य सोख ले ।
स्वाति बूँद ! चातक को आत्मलीन तू कर ले !
ओ वरिष्ठ ! ओ वरदे ! वर ले !

'अज्ञेय'

O My Other Self

Today once more I awaken love
Opening all shut doors,
I bathe every corner of this
Stifled house of gold
In golden sunlight.
You who are mine, Who is in me
In the densest denseness
Who is unique
From afar, from the district,
From the country, from time,
From the base, from the bottomless,
From the earth, from the ocean,
From the universe,
From the core of the eternal brightness,
I, possessed, my being full of you,
Sacrificing myself to you
O my other self
O unique love,
O richness of love,
Today, once more,
I beckon you

And, whoever I am, whatever I have known,
Whatever I have lived, owned, is mine,
Wealth, possession, Every bit of it
I dedicate to you.

The mountain peaks
Whose snow covered deft fingers
From a choiceless direction
Have spread this infinite light
On to the startled plane of my consciousness
Such is your voice, spread like a wave of song
And my blissful memory comes alive.
I have touched you
You, filled in my grasp
Have filtered through my closed fingers and flowed
Moment, every moment full, clear, experienced.
I have kissed you
And my every blood cell has kept the
Warm, red, embossed
Impression of every kiss
Oh! But I have not known you

No! I have merely known you
I have not seen ever,
Or heard or touched ever,
Have not tasted the essence of your being
O self-evident proof!
I have known,
Merely known you.

I could not see
My vision was limited,
Because you contain a world in you,

I could not touch:
My touch remained incomplete
Because you are liquid, airy
I could not recognize you
Because you are mysterious, seductive.

But yes, I could capture it,
Capture it, experience it
Because the experience of life
Catches you in a flash of lightning
Like a tight claw.
Strong:
A net inescapable
Nothing, nowhere, never
Can elude experience

Life experience: a claw wherein
I too have come to be caught along with you
A net in which I too have become trapped with you
Life experience:
One mill. One fulcrum
A full stop like a mountain
Brought about by the turning tide of the wave time
One furnace, one self-glowing experience

I have merely known you,
Only known you,
I have known you,
Have worshipped you without thinking of the fruit,
Have constantly remembered you.

And I have seen
And my memory
Has given flesh to the images in my mind's eye
I have listened
And my compulsive memory in a fainting fit
Has entwined all your words
I smelt and memory
Seeped all smells in the
One fragrance of spring,
I have touched:
And my knowledge has given
That unique shape
To countless idols of illusion
That shape which only I have recognized
That which I alone have loved.
I have kissed,
And oh the taste of my being
Recognition has taken me to that river
Whose nectarine, unstained, matchless stream
Quenches my thirst.

Yes, I have known you,
I know you, I recognize you,
My companion,
And I do not forget, I can never forget!
I do not forget
Can never forget,
And I do not want to get scattered.
Today I sacrifice myself to you, my beloved.

That which I have to say in this burning moment
Till the sacred flame glows on my tongue,

I should say it:
Let the one who lights my flame
Be my witness!

O sacred one!
O visible!
Inimitable!
O self-established
Hear my vow:
I have touched and I have been touched;
I have kissed and I have been kissed;
I am the conqueror and I have been conquered;
I am and I have been given;
I have lived, and that which has been taken from inside of me
I have been erased, won over, lost
I have been extracted, dissolved
I am immortal, eternal.

Having recognized my goal,
I have walked forth in the light,
Determined; focused.
Wherever I formed familiarities
I moved on;
Maternal love turned me
I snapped the thread.
I erased every step,
Destroyed every path,
Doused the flame of every candle,
Going forward in the darkness,
I attached my heart to you.

O my journey mate
We ourselves are the ocean,
And its ends
Because we have crossed it.

O my companion,
We ourselves are that lucid transparent water
That we drink palms full
Again and again,
With thirst, with satisfaction,
Happily, curiously
Because we ourselves are the wetness
That completes it.

O my soulmate,
Touch my hand:
So I can offer sacrifice
We are the worshippers,
We are the sacrificial fire,
And we are the co-offerings in it.

O my unsatisfied, unquenchable flame,
The one who sacrificed me,
O my offering,
Come consume me
The way I have consumed you
We are co-dependent, because we are sustaining
Co-existing

O co-born, co-fortunate,
Eternally wedded,
Co- liberator,
Soulmate, bestower of fortune.

O auspicious one
My source of lightning,
The drop of water on a lotus leaf,
The star of my eyes,
O my pole star, O mischevious
O hard attained,
The pearl extracted from every wave,
O reflection of the world
Now, envelop this shell in your self,
Absorb this scene.
O elixir, consume the alchemist!
O greatest! Bless me, make a blessing of me!

Agyeya

Contributed By:

Dr L. M. Singhvi - is a Jain and Indic scholar and the chairperson of the High Level Committee on Indian Diaspora. He was also the Indian high commissioner to London from 1991-1997. He was a member of the Rajya Sabha, chaired the Indian national committee for abolition of the death penalty, and is the past president of the Asian Human Rights Conference. A constitutional lawyer of considerable distinction, Dr Singhvi is India's longest serving envoy to the Court of St James. A fellowship in his name is conferred on students at the University of Wales.

Speak Gently 62

Speak Gently! It is better far
To rule by love, than fear;
Speak gently! Let no harsh words mar
The good we might do here!

Speak gently!Love doth whisper low
The vows that true hearts bind;
And gently Friendship's accents flow;
Affection's voice is kind.

Speak gently to the little child,
It's love be sure to gain.
Teach it in accents soft and mild;
It may not long remain.

Speak gently to the young, for they
Will have enough to bear–
Pass though this life as best they may,
'T is full of anxious care!

Speak gently to the aged one,
Grieve not the care-worn heart.
The course of life is nearly run,
Let such in peace depart.

Speak gently, kindly to the poor,
Let no harsh tone be heard,
They have enough they must endure,
Without an unkind word.

Speak gently to the erring – know,
They may have toiled in vain;
Perchance unkindness made them so;
Oh, win them back again!

Speak gently!He who gave his life
To bend man's stubborn will,
When elements were in fierce strife,
Said to them, 'Peace, be still.'

Speak gently!'tis a little thing,
Dropped in the heart's deep well
The good, the joy which it may bring
Long days to come shall tell.

David Bates

Contributed By:

Brinda Somaya - Architect and conservationist Brinda Somaya believes that development and progress must proceed without straining the cultural and historic environment. Her oeuvre spans large corporate, industrial and institutional buildings, public spaces, which she has rebuilt and often reinvented as pavements, parks and plazas. For this, she has won several awards. She is a founder trustee of the Hecar Foundation, which organised a conference and exhibition on the work of women architects, with a focus on south Asia. She has been a member of the Urban Heritage Conservation Committee and Mumbai's initiative for the protection and improvement of streets and public spaces. Mrs Somaya's work has been exhibited in the USA, UK & Japan. She has also served on juries, and lectured extensively overseas.

'After my mother died I was rummaging amongst her old papers trying to put things into order, so to say, when I came across a Lion's Table Diary for 1943. The first page had, in her handwriting, her initials and The Book of Truth written across the empty page.

She was thirty years old, unmarried and a very liberated woman for her time. On turning the pages, I found them filled with poems and sayings. As I read what she had written more than fifty years earlier I found one, which became my favourite because it truly represented her life. I do not know the author, perhaps I will know someday. My mother did speak kindly to all. The day she died the first two people who came in together to offer their condolences could not have been more different. One was an industrialist from one of the biggest business houses in India and the other our "jamadar" Narayan. They both arrived carrying different sized bouquets of flowers. Narayan was crying. That was my mother…..She "spoke gently" to one and all.'

Man's Testament 63

Question not, but live and labour
Till yon goal be won,
Helping every feeble neighbour,
Seeking help from none;
Life is mostly froth and bubble,
Two things stand like stone,
Kindness in another's trouble,
Courage in your own.

Adam Lindsay Gordon

Contributed By:

Soli J. Sorabjee - is the former attorney general of India. He was conferred the Padam Vibhushan, the second highest civilian award of the nation, in March 2002. The legal mind is also a dedicated campaigner for human rights.

(34)

Let only that little be left of me whereby I may name thee my all.
Let only that little be left of my will whereby I may feel thee on every side, and come to thee in everything, and offer to thee my love every moment.
Let only that little be left of me whereby I may never hide thee.
Let only that little of my fetters be left whereby I am bound with thy will, and thy purpose is carried out in my life and that is the fetter of thy love.

(35)

Where the mind is without fear and the head is held high;
Where knowledge is free;
Where the world has not been broken up into fragments by narrow domestic walls;
Where words come out from the depth of truth;
Where tireless striving stretches its arms towards perfection;
Where the clear stream of reason has not lost its way into the dreary desert sand of dead habit;
Where the mind is led forward by thee into ever-widening thought and action
Into that heaven of freedom, my Father, let my country awake.

(36)

This is my prayer to thee, my Lord strike, strike at the root of penury in my heart.
Give me the strength lightly to bear my joys and sorrows.
Give me the strength to make my love fruitful in service.
Give me the strength never to disown the poor or bend my knees before insolent might.

Give me the strength to raise my mind high above daily trifles.
And give me the strength to surrender my strength to thy will with love.

Rabindranath Tagore

Contributed By:

Sharmila Tagore - Actress Sharmila Tagore's versatile filmography spans Satyajit Ray films, Bollywood extravaganzas, classic social dramas, and Indian parallel cinema. She made her debut in Hindi films as an incarnation of the Goddess Kali in Ray's film *Devi*. After this successful initiation, she went on to act in *Aradhana* with Rajesh Khanna. The award winning actress married India's former cricket captain, the Nawab of Pataudi, Mansoor Ali Khan.

Ode to a Nightingale 65

My heart aches, and a drowsy numbness pains
My sense, as though of hemlock I had drunk,
Or emptied some dull opiate to the drains
One minute past, and Lethe-wards had sunk:
'Tis not through envy of thy happy lot,
But being too happy in thine happiness,
That thou, light-winged Dryad of the trees,
In some melodious plot
Of beechen green, and shadows numberless,
Singest of summer in full-throated ease.

O for a draught of vintage! that hath been
Cool'd a long age in the deep-delved earth,
Tasting of Flora and the country-green,
Dance, and Provençal song, and sunburnt mirth!
O for a beaker full of the warm South!
Full of the true, the blushful Hippocrene,
With beaded bubbles winking at the brim,
And purple-stained mouth;
That I might drink, and leave the world unseen,
And with thee fade away into the forest dim:

Fade far away, dissolve, and quite forget
What thou among the leaves hast never known,
The weariness, the fever, and the fret
Here, where men sit and hear each other groan;
Where palsy shakes a few, sad, last grey hairs,
Where youth grows pale, and spectre-thin, and dies;
Where but to think is to be full of sorrow
And leaden-eyed despairs,
Where beauty cannot keep her lustrous eyes,
Or new Love pine at them beyond to-morrow.

Away! away! for I will fly to thee,
  Not charioted by Bacchus and his pards,
But on the viewless wings of Poesy,
  Though the dull brain perplexes and retards:
Already with thee! tender is the night,
  And haply the Queen-Moon is on her throne,
    Cluster'd around by all her starry Fays
      But here there is no light,
  Save what from heaven is with the breezes blown
    Through verdurous glooms and winding mossy ways.

I cannot see what flowers are at my feet,
  Nor what soft incense hangs upon the boughs,
But, in embalmed darkness, guess each sweet
  Wherewith the seasonable month endows
The grass, the thicket, and the fruit-tree wild;
  White hawthorn, and the pastoral eglantine;
    Fast-fading violets cover'd up in leaves;
      And mid-May's eldest child,
  The coming musk-rose, full of dewy wine,
    The murmurous haunt of flies on summer eves.

Darkling I listen; and, for many a time
  I have been half in love with easeful Death,
Call'd him soft names in many a mused rhyme,
  To take into the air my quiet breath;
Now more than ever seems it rich to die,
  To cease upon the midnight with no pain,
    While thou art pouring forth thy soul abroad
      In such an ecstasy!
  Still wouldst thou sing, and I have ears in vain --
    To thy high requiem become a sod.

Thou wast not born for death, immortal Bird!
  No hungry generations tread thee down;

The voice I hear this passing night was heard
  In ancient days by emperor and clown:
Perhaps the self-same song that found a path
  Through the sad heart of Ruth, when, sick for home,
    She stood in tears amid the alien corn;
        The same that oft-times hath
  Charm'd magic casements, opening on the foam
    Of perilous seas, in faery lands forlorn.

Forlorn! the very word is like a bell
  To toll me back from thee to my sole self!
Adieu! the fancy cannot cheat so well
  As she is famed to do, deceiving elf.
Adieu! adieu! thy plaintive anthem fades
  Past the near meadows, over the still stream,
    Up the hill-side; and now 'tis buried deep
        In the next valley-glades:
  Was it a vision, or a waking dream?
    Fled is that music:—do I wake or sleep?

John Keats

Contributed By:

Tarun Tahiliani - A graduate from Wharton Business School, he is now one of India's leading fashion designers. He has continued to present exclusive, well attended and highly publicised shows in major cities all over the world.

'My favorite of all times is "Ode to a Nightingale". For one, I love the murky night and the image of the bird spotted through "verdurous glooms and winding mossy ways". The soothing rhythm, the play of words, the images they conjure up without being in rhyme!... and finally, that it is an ode, a great song of love.'

Reeds of Innocence 66

Piping down the valleys wild,
Piping songs of pleasant glee,
On a cloud I saw a child,
And he laughing said to me:

'Pipe a song about a Lamb!'
So I piped with merry cheer.
'Piper, pipe that song again;'
So I piped: he wept to hear.

'Drop thy pipe, thy happy pipe;
Sing thy songs of happy cheer!'
So I sung the same again,
While he wept with joy to hear.

'Piper, sit thee down and write
In a book that all may read.'
So he vanish'd from my sight;
And I pluck'd a hollow reed,

And I made a rural pen,
And I stain'd the water clear,
And I wrote my happy songs
Every child may joy to hear.

William Blake

Contributed By:

Raveena Tandon - is an award winning film and television actress, recently turned producer. Committed to child rights and the cause of underprivileged children, she has been the brand ambassador of CRY.

'I like this poem because it epitomizes the joy there is in making children happy.'

Perhaps, may be because of you,
But cricket to me,
Dear Sachin, is no more a game, but a poem
A lyrical poem!…
Intensity, concentration, spontaneity,
Moods and tensions and form,
Rhythm and movement and composition …
And flashes of imagination and talent
When the strokes go across the boundaries …

And of all the things that string of uncertainty
Hanging all the time
Making moment of every movement
A creative moment and a challenge …
What else can all this be
If not a lyric on the playground?

Hence, this vocabulary
Rushing unto me
As I sit down, dear Sachin,
To describe your game!

Professor Ramesh Tendulkar

Contributed By:

Sachin Tendulkar - is to cricket what Michael Jordan is to basketball. Debuting at sixteen, Sachin is one of the world's most brilliant cricketers. The first batsman to score 10,000 runs in one-day cricket, he can certainly be credited with raising the bar for cricketers globally.

Dulce Et Decorum Est 68

Bent double, like old beggars under sacks,
Knock-kneed, coughing like hags, we cursed through sludge,
Till on the haunting flares we turned our backs,
And towards our distant rest began to trudge.
Men marched asleep. Many had lost their boots,
But limped on, blood-shod. All went lame; all blind;
Drunk with fatigue; deaf even to the hoots
Of tired, outstripped Five-Nines that dropped behind.

Gas! Gas! Quick, boys!–An ecstasy of fumbling,
Fitting the clumsy helmets just in time;
But someone still was yelling out and stumbling
And flound'ring like a man in fire or lime.–
Dim through the misty panes and thick green light,
As under a green sea, I saw him drowning.
In all my dreams before my helpless sight
He plunges at me, guttering, choking, drowning.

If in some smothering dreams, you too could pace
Behind the wagon that we flung him in,
And watch the white eyes writhing in his face,
His hanging face, like a devil's sick of sin;
If you could hear, at every jolt, the blood
Come gargling from the froth-corrupted lungs
Obscene as cancer, bitter as the cud
Of vile, incurable sores on innocent tongues,--
My friend, you would not tell with such high zest
To children ardent for some desperate glory,
The old Lie: Dulce et Decorum est
Pro patria mori.

Wilfred Owen

Contributed By:

Shashi Tharoor - is the under-secretary-general for communication and public information for the United Nations. He is the author of numerous articles, short stories, books and commentaries and is the winner of several journalism and literary awards, including the Commonwealth Writer's Prize.

'There are many reasons why this poem is special to me: its extraordinary evocation of the horror and the pity of war, without mawkishness or sentimentality; its searing subversion of the warrior myths sought to be imparted to the young in mottoes like "Dulce et decorum est pro patria mori" [Latin for "it is sweet and proper to die for one's country"]; its brilliant literary quality, all the more so for having been written under gunfire; and the tragic futility of the wasted life of the poet, Wilfred Owen, whose death as a young soldier in World War I deprived the English-speaking world of the pen of one whose greatness is unquestionable.'

हरी भरी दूब पर 69

हरी-हरी दूब पर
ओस की बूँदें
अभी थीं,
अब नहीं हैं ।
ऐसी खुशियाँ
जो हमेशा हमारा साथ दें
कभी नहीं थीं
कभी नहीं हैं ।

क्वाँर की कोख से
फूटा बाल सूर्य,
जब पूरब की गोद में
पाँव फैलाने लगा,
तो मेरी बगीची का
पत्ता-पत्ता जगमगाने लगा,
मैं उगते सूर्य को नमस्कार करूँ
या उसके ताप से भाप बनी,
ओस की बूँदों को ढूँढूँ?

सूर्य एक सत्य है
जिसे झुठलाया नहीं जा सकता
मगर ओस भी तो एक सच्चाई है
यह बात अलग है कि ओस क्षणिक है
क्यों न मैं क्षण-क्षण को जीऊँ?
कण-कण में बिखरे सौन्दर्य को पीऊँ?

सूर्य तो फिर भी उगेगा,
धूप तो फिर भी खिलेगी,
लेकिन मेरी बगीची की,
हरी-हरी दूब पर,
ओस की बूँद
हर मौसम में नहीं मिलेगी ।

श्री अटल बिहारी वाजपेयी

On the Soft Green Grass

Dew drops
On the soft green grass
Were there a moment ago
No longer.
Everlasting happiness
Never existed
Anywhere.

When the sun
Rose from the womb of the
Cold October night
Stretched his legs in the lap
Of the eastern sky
Every leaf in my little garden
Wore lustre on its tips.
Shall I pray to the rising sun? Or
Search for the dew drops
Banished by his heat?

The sun is a reality
You cannot deny.
But the dew drop too
Is a reality, isn't it?
It's another matter it
Exists only for a moment.
Shouldn't I too live
Each moment? Enjoy the beauty in
Each fragment?

The sun will rise again.
Of course, there'll be
Sunshine all over again.
But the dew drop
On the soft green grass
In my little garden
Will not be there
In all seasons.

Atal Bihari Vajpayee

Contributed By:

Atal Bihari Vajpayee - was prime minister of India for a fortnight in May 1996 and again from March 1998 to May 2004. A Member of Parliament since 1957 for constituencies in Uttar Pradesh, Gujarat, Madhya Pradesh and Delhi, he was India's external affairs minister from March 1977 to July 1979. Shri Vajpayee's published works include collections of poems *Kaidi Kaviraj Ki Kundalian* (written in jail during the Emergency) and *Amar Aag Hai*. He is known to be a voracious reader and is fond of Indian music and dance.

'I liked this poem because it looks at the beauty of small things in life. We generally tend to look at the big things of life, like the rising sun, which symbolises power. But it is also important to take care of the small and transitory aspects of life, such as the dew drops that the rising sun causes to disappear. Sensitivity towards the poor, caring for the weak, greeting a child with a smile or savouring the ordinary joys of life - our fleeting moments should be filled with these. This is what the poem seeks to convey.'

Ulysses 70

It little profits that an idle king,
By this still hearth, among these barren crags,
Match'd with an aged wife, I mete and dole
Unequal laws unto a savage race,
That hoard, and sleep, and feed, and know not me.
I cannot rest from travel: I will drink
Life to the lees: all times I have enjoyed
Greatly, have suffer'd greatly, both with those
That loved me, and alone; on shore, and when
Through scudding drifts the rainy Hyades
Vexed the dim sea: I am become a name;
For always roaming with a hungry heart
Much have I seen and known;–cities of men
And manners, climates, councils, governments,
Myself not least, but honoured of them all;–
And drunk delight of battle with my peers,
Far on the ringing plains of windy Troy.
I am part of all that I have met;
Yet all experience is an arch wherethrough
Gleams that untravell'd world, whose margin fades
For ever and for ever when I move.
How dull it is to pause, to make an end,
To rust unburnished, not to shine in use!
As though to breath were life. Life piled on life
Were all too little, and of one to me
Little remains; but every hour is saved
From that eternal silence, something more,
A bringer of new things; and vile it were
For some three suns to store and hoard myself,
And this gray spirit yearning in desire

To follow knowledge like a sinking star,
Beyond the utmost bound of human thought.
This is my son, mine own Telemachus,
To whom I leave the sceptre and the isle,–
Well-loved of me, discerning to fulfill
This labour, by slow prudence to make mild
A rugged people, and through soft degrees
Subdue them to the useful and the good.
Most blameless is he, centred in the sphere
Of common duties, decent not to fail
In offices of tenderness, and pay
Meet adoration to my household gods,
When I am gone. He works his work, I mine.

There lies the port; the vessel puffs her sail:
There gloom the dark broad seas. My mariners,
Souls that have toil'd, and wrought, and thought with me-
That ever with a frolic welcome took
The thunder and the sunshine, and opposed
Free hearts, free foreheads,–you and I are old;
Old age had yet his honour and his toil;
Death closes all; but something ere the end,
Some work of noble note, may yet be done,
Not unbecoming men that strove with Gods.
The lights begin to twinkle from the rocks:
The long day wanes; the slow moon climbs; the deep
Moans round with many voices. Come, my friends,
'Tis not too late to seek a newer world.
Push off, and sitting well in order smite
The sounding furrows; for my purpose holds
To sail beyond the sunset, and the baths
Of all the western stars, until I die.

It may be that the gulfs will wash us down;
It may be we shall touch the Happy Isles,
And see the great Achilles, whom we knew.
Tho' much is taken, much abides; and though
We are not now that strength which in old days
Moved earth and heaven; that which we are, we are;
One equal-temper of heroic hearts,
Made weak by time and fate, but strong in will
To strive, to seek, to find, and not to yield.

Alfred Tennyson

Contributed By:

Dr Fareed Zakaria - is the editor of *Newsweek International*, having previously been editor of *Foreign Affairs*. He has published *The Future of Freedom: Illiberal Use of Democracy at Home and Abroad*, a book making the case that individual liberty, not democracy, is the prerequisite for a nation's economic and political growth. Dr Zakaria also authored *From Wealth to Power*, which examines America's role on the world stage. Fareed Zakaria was educated at Yale and Harvard, where he received his Ph.D in International Relations. Often described as 'the most influential foreign policy adviser of his generation', he presents his own TV show, *Foreign Exchange*, and serves as a regular member of the roundtable on the ABC television show, *This Week*. Zakaria has written for the *New York Times*, the *Wall Street Journal*, the *Washington Post* and the *New Yorker*. And, in a refreshing departure, he was the wine columnist for *Slate*.

'I like poems for their sounds. Poetry is music. It must ring in your ears, capture your imagination, thrill your senses.

The love of poetry is an emotional and spiritual experience more than it is an intellectual one. When I think of this poem, I think of the memorable turns of phrase scattered throughout it:

"I am a part of all that I have met; I will drink life to the lees; For always roaming with a hungry heart; To follow knowledge like a sinking star, The long day wanes, the slow moon climbs; To sail beyond the sunset." Then there is the meaning. Ulysses is the interior monologue of an aging king who has had a full, rich life. He is a wonderfully human character: angry, sad, and honest. But above all else, he believes in a purposeful life,even though he has little left of it. Tennyson once explained that this poem expressed "his feelings about the need of going forward, and braving the struggle of life." Whenever we despair, think we cannot achieve anything, That important actions are for someone else to do, or have already been done, think of this poem, the dying king, and his will to live a strenuous life to the end. And think of these haunting last lines."Tho' much is taken, much abides; and tho' We are not now that strength which in the old days Moved earth and heaven; that which we are, we are;One equal temper of heroic hearts, made weak by time and fate, but strong in will; To strive, to seek, to find, and not to yield."

To strive, to seek, to find, and not to yield - Not a bad motto to live by.'

All You Who Sleep Tonight 71

All you who sleep tonight
Far from the ones you love,
No hand to left or right
And emptiness above —

Know that you aren't alone
The whole world shares your tears,
Some for two nights or one,
And some for all their years.

Vikram Seth

Contributed By:

Dr R. A. Mashelkar - is an eminent scientist. As director general of the Council of Scientific and Industrial Research (CSIR), the largest chain of industrial research and development institutions in the world, he has made significant contributions to R & D and is an advocate of patenting. His fellowship of the Royal Society is an honour shared by only thirty-five Indian scientists and engineers in over three centuries.

'I always like lectures, write-ups, poems, etc., which end in hope, inspite of the problems that may appear to be insurmountable that are being addressed. The poem, as you see, belongs to this category.'

I wish I lived in a caravan,
With a horse to drive, like a peddler-man!
Where he comes from nobody knows,
Or where he goes to, but on he goes!

His caravan has windows two,
And a chimney of tin, that the smoke comes through;
He has a wife, with a baby brown,
And they go riding from town to town.

Chairs to mend, and delf to sell!
He clashes the basins like a bell;
Tea-trays, baskets ranged in order,
Plates, with alphabets round the border!

The roads are brown, and the sea is green,
But his house is like a bathing-machine;
The world is round, and he can ride,
Rumble and slash, to the other side!

With the peddler-man I should like to roam,
And write a book when I came home;
All the people would read my book,
Just like the Travels of Captain Cook!

William Brighty Rands

Contributed By:

Zubin Mehta - At the age of eighteen, Zubin Mehta abandoned medical studies to attend the Academy of Music in Vienna. Just seven years later, he was conducting both the Vienna and Berlin Philharmonics. In 1978, this maestro became the music director of the New York Philharmonic Orchestra. During his thirteen years in New York, he conducted over 1,000 concerts, and held the position longer than any music director in the Orchestra's modern history. He has also been the principal conductor of major orchestras in Los Angeles, Israel and Florence. Famously, in 1991, the maestro concluded his tenure in New York with three performances celebrating the 100th anniversary of Carnegie Hall. A memorable occasion for Mr Mehta was when, in 1994, he brought the Israel Philharmonic Orchestra to India. Conducting in Bombay and New Delhi, he helped bridge a political gap that had prevented performances in India for three decades.

'It was the first one I learnt in school as a boy, and brings back happy memories. I find it soul stirring, the way I do Western Classical music.'

Stopping by Woods on a Snowy Evening 73

Whose woods these are I think I know.
His house is in the village though;
He will not see me stopping here
To watch his woods fill up with snow.
My little horse must think it queer
To stop without a farmhouse near
Between the woods and frozen lake
The darkest evening of the year.
He gives his harness bells a shake
To ask if there is some mistake.
The only other sound's the sweep
Of easy wind and downy flake.
The woods are lovely, dark and deep.
But I have promises to keep,
And miles to go before I sleep,
And miles to go before I sleep.

Robert Frost

Contributed By:

Mario Miranda - A well-loved cartoonist and an institution in his own right, Mario Miranda's artwork comes straight from the heart. The Wordsworthian equivalent of caricature, Mr Miranda is an itinerant who uses his travels as inspiration for his art. Central to his drawings is his sense of humour and his ability to extricate hilarity from a situation as dire as a funeral. Mr Miranda's work has featured in restaurant murals, books, newspapers ad infinitum.

'The winter setting in the poem is beautifully written, especially the last two lines which are extremely moving and pertinent.'

K. C. Pant - was the deputy chairman of the planning commission for the government of India. He is also chairman of the task force on infrastructure and member, National Security Council. He has been actively involved in resolving the long-standing dispute between India and Pakistan over Kashmir.

'The last four lines of the poem capture a mood to which each one of us can relate; besides, they have a special meaning for me.'

Youth is not a time of life; it is a state of mind; it is not a matter of rosy cheeks, red lips and supple knees; it is a matter of the will, a quality of the imagination, a vigor of the emotions; it is the freshness of the deep springs of life.

Youth means a temperamental predominance of courage over timidity of the appetite, for adventure over the love of ease. This often exists in a man of sixty more than a boy of twenty. Nobody grows old merely by a number of years. We grow old by deserting our ideals.

Years may wrinkle the skin, but to give up enthusiasm wrinkles the soul. Worry, fear, self-distrust bows the heart and turns the spirit back to dust.

Whether sixty or sixteen, there is in every human being's heart the lure of wonder, the unfailing child-like appetite of what's next, and the joy of the game of living. In the center of your heart and my heart there is a wireless station; so long as it receives messages of beauty, hope, cheer, courage and power from men and from the Infinite, so long are you young.

When the aerials are down, and your spirit is covered with snows of cynicism and the ice of pessimism, then you are grown old, even at twenty, but as long as your aerials are up, to catch the waves of optimism, there is hope you may die young at eighty.

Samuel Ullman

Contributed By:

Sunil Bharti Mittal - is the chairman and group managing director, Bharti Enterprises, India. He is a graduate from Punjab University. Originally belonging to a small town, he founded his telecom empire in 1976.

'It is very easy to rest on one's laurels and this poem pushes you out from your comfort zone to seek higher challenges in life. There is only one life and Much to accomplish. This poem is highly energizing and motivating.'

Merrow Down 75

I

There runs a road by Merrow Down –
  A grassy track today it is –
An hour out of Guildford town,
  Above the river Wey it is.
Here, when they heard the horse-bells ring,
  The ancient Britons dressed and rode
To watch the dark Phoenicians bring
  Their goods along the Western Road.
Yes, here, or hereabouts, they met
  To hold their racial talks and such –
To barter beads for Whitby jet,
  And tin for gay shell torques and such.
But long and long before that time
  (When bison used to roam on it)
Did Taffy and her Daddy climb
  That Down, and had their home on it.
Then beavers built in Broadstonebrook
  And made a swamp where Bramley stands;
And bears from Shere would come and look
  For Taffimai where Shamley stands.
The Way, that Taffy called Wagai,
Was more than six times bigger then;
And all the Tribe of Tegumai
  They cut a noble figure then!

II

Of all the Tribe of Tegumai
  Who cut that figure, none remain –
On Merrow Down the cuckoos cry–

The silence and the sun remain.
But as the faithful years return
And hearts unwounded sing again,
Comes Taffy dancing through the fern
To lead the Surrey spring again.
Her brows are bound with bracken-fronds
And golden elf-locks fly above;
Her eyes are bright as diamonds
And bluer than the sky above.
In mocassins and deer-skin cloak,
Unfearing, free and fair she flits,
And lights her little damp-wood smoke
To show her Daddy where she flits.
For far–oh, very far behind,
So far she cannot call to him,
Comes Tegumai alone to find
The daughter that was all to him!

Rudyard Kipling

Contributed By:

Dom Moraes - The late Dom Moraes was Mumbai's leading poet. When he was nineteen, his first book of poems, *A Beginning*, won the Hawthornden Prize, which was, at the time, a highly coveted literary award. He went on to publish several more anthologies and twenty-three novels, including a biography, *Mrs. Gandhi,* and two memoirs: *Never at Home* and *My Son's Father.* In 1971, he became editor of the *Asia Magazine* and in 1976 he joined the UN. He returned to India in 1979 and continued to write. Mr Moraes lived in Mumbai until his death in 2004.

'I would say my favourite poem, at least when I was a child, was "Merrow Down" by Rudyard Kipling. It has some history in it and I was then familiar with the part of England it describes. Rudyard Kipling has been described as the poet of Empire and certainly his early work justifies that description. But as he grew older and became mature (this took a long time) he became a better poet. His only daughter died very young and Kipling mourned her for many years. The last stanza of the poem seems very tragic to me .'

Maru Satakam 76

A frown spelled wrath
And silence could inhibit
A smile was a plea
And a look an offering.
Such was our love. Look how it lies in ruins.
You lie at my feet, seeking forgiveness
And I cannot untangle myself from my anger.

Amaru

(Translated from the Sanskrit by Mukund Lath)

Contributed By:

Madhavi Mudgal - was enthralled by music and dance from a very young age and trained in Bharata Natyam and Kathak. Later she adopted Odissi as her preferred medium, under Guru Hare Krishna Bahera. She teaches, performs and conducts workshops on the art of Odissi. Her command over the nritta or purely ornamental aspect of Odissi combines with her subtle abhinaya (the expressional aspect) and musical knowledge, enhancing the uniqueness of her performances. She has received the Sanskriti Award, the Padma Shri and the Sangeet Natak Akademi Award for her contribution to the world of Indian dance.

'I came across this poem while making a selection for a special dance composition. The poet, Amaru, is one of the most celebrated of Sanskrit poets who wrote Muktakas, short four-line poems. Love was a favourite theme of Muktaka poets and Amaru, one of its greatest masters. He lived just after the Gupta age during the 6th - 7th century AD and he is perhaps the only Sanskrit poet sensitive to the tragedy of love ending in indifference.'

ये बच्चा कैसा बच्चा है ... 77

ये बच्चा कैसा बच्चा है
ये बच्चा काला काला सा, ये काला सा मटियाला सा
ये बच्चा भूखा भूखा सा, ये बच्चा सूखा सूखा सा

ये बच्चा किसका बच्चा है
ये बच्चा कैसा बच्चा है जो रेत पे तनहा बैठा है
न उसके पेट में रोटी है, न उसके तन पर कपड़ा है
न उसके सर पर टोपी है, न उसके पैर में जूता है
न उसके पास खिलौनों में, कोई भालू है कोई घोड़ा है
न उसका जी बहलाने को कोई लोरी है कोई झूला है
न इसकी जेब में धेला है, न इसके हाथ में पैसा है
न इसके अम्मी अब्बू हैं न इसकी आपा ख़ाला है
ये सारे जग में तनहा है, ये बच्चा कैसा बच्चा है

ये सहरा कैसा सहरा है
न इस सहरा में बादल हैं, न इस सहरा में बरखा है
न इस सहरा में बाली है, न इस सहरा में ख़ोशा है
न इस सहरा में सब्ज़ा है, न इस सहरा में साया है
ये सहरा भूख का सहरा है, ये सहरा मौत का सहरा है

ये बच्चा कैसे बैठा है ये बच्चा कब से बैठा है
ये बच्चा क्या क्या पूछता है, ये बच्चा क्या कुछ कहता है

ये दुनिया कैसी दुनिया है, ये दुनिया किसकी दुनिया है
इस दुनिया के कुछ टुकड़ों में कहीं फूल खिले कहीं सब्ज़ा है
कहीं बादल घिर घिर आते हैं, कहीं चश्मा है कहीं दरिया है
कहीं ऊँचे महल अटारियाँ हैं, कहीं महफिल है कहीं मेला है
कहीं कपड़ों के बाज़ार सजे, ये रेशम है ये दीबा है
कहीं गल्ले के अम्बार लगे, सब गेहूँ धान मोहैय्या है
कहीं दौलत के सन्दूक भरे, हाँ ताँबा सोना रुपा है
तुम जो माँगो सो हाज़िर है, तुम जो चाहो सो मिलता है

इस भूख के दुख की दुनिया में ये कैसा सुख का सपना है
वो किस धरती के टुकड़े हैं, ये किस दुनिया का हिस्सा है
हम जिस आदम के बेटे हैं ये उस आदम का बेटा है
ये आदम एक ही आदम है, वो गोरा है या काला है
ये धरती एक ही धरती है ये दुनिया एक ही दुनिया है
सब इक दाता के बन्दे हैं, सब बन्दों का इक दाता है
कुछ पूरब पच्छिम फर्क नहीं, इस धरती पर हक़ सबका है

ये तनहा बच्चा बेचारा, ये बच्चा जो यहाँ बैठा है
इस बच्चे की कहीं भूख मिटे, क्या मुश्किल है ? हो सकता है
इस बच्चे को कहीं दूध मिले, हाँ दूध यहाँ बहुतेरा है
इस बच्चे का कोई तन ढाँके, क्या कपड़ों का यहां तोड़ा है
इस बच्चे को कोई गोद में ले, इंसान जो अब तक ज़िन्दा है
फिर देखें कैसा बच्चा है, ये कितना प्यारा बच्चा है
इस जग में सब कुछ रब का है, जो रब का है वो सब का है
सब अपने हैं कोई ग़ैर नहीं, हर चीज़ में सब का साझा है
जो बढ़ता है, जो उगता है, वो दाना है या मेवा है
जो कपड़ा है जो कम्बल है, जो चाँदी है जो सोना है
वो सारा है इस बच्चे का, जो तेरा है जो मेरा है
ये बच्चा किसका बच्चा है ?
ये बच्चा सब का बच्चा है ।

इब्ने इंशा

This Child, What Child Is This…

This child, what child is this,
Dark is this child, dark and quite dusty
Hungry is this child and weak is he.

Whose child is this
What child is this, sitting alone on the sand,
No food in his belly, no clothes on his back,
No cap on his head nor shoes on his feet.
He does not have toys, no teddies or horses
No one to sing him lullabies or to swing him
To keep him occupied.
Not a single coin in his pocket or money in hand
He has neither father nor mother, sister or aunt.
All alone in this wide world, what child is this.

What a desert this is
This desert has no clouds or rain
No buds nor ears of grain
No greenery or shadow,
This desert is one of hunger, this desert is one of death.

How is this child sitting and since when,
What does this child ask,
What does this child say?

What a world is this and whose is it
Flowers bloom in some parts and
There is greenery in others.
Some parts are overcast with clouds,
Some have fountains, others rivers
Some have tall palaces and rooftops,
Gatherings and fairs
Silk and satins in marketplaces of clothes.
Heaps of grain in some parts, rice and wheat available everywhere
Boxes filled with untold wealth, gold and copper and silver.
All yours for the asking, all slaves of your will

What a dream this is, in a world filled with the pain of hunger,
What parts of the earth are those, what slice of the world is this.
The Adam we are sons of, is his father too
That Adam is the only Adam, not white or black
This earth is just one earth, this world just one world,
All followers of one god, with one god for all.
No difference between east or west,
With equal rights over earth for all.

This poor lonely child, this child who sits here
Wipe away his hunger, why not? It is possible.
Can he get some milk, yes, milk is in plenty here
If someone were to clothe him, is there a lack of clothes?
If someone were to take him in, that humanity that is still alive,
Then we would see what child this is,
How sweet a child is he.
Everything in this world is god's
And what is god's is for all.
Everyone is our own, and in everything we have a share.
Whatever grows, whatever germinates, berry or fruit
Cloth or blanket, silver or gold
Everything is this child's, whatever is yours or mine
Whose child is this?
This child is ours.

Ibne Insha

Contributed By:

Shubha Mudgal - One of the most versatile and popular Hindustani musicians, Shubha Mudgal is among India's most imaginative and adventurous female vocalists. A disciple of Jitendra Abhisheki, she developed her innovative style rather than adhering to a particular gharana and encourages her students to do the same. The classical singer has also succeeded in the pop genre and has won recognition as a composer. She is highly acclaimed for her repertoire of medieval devotional poetry and she wrote music and essayed a cameo role in Mira Nair's *Kama Sutra*.

Banalata Sen **78**

Long I have been a wanderer of this world,
Many a night,
My route lay across the sea of Ceylon somewhat winding to
The seas of Malaya.
I was in the dim world of Bimbisar and Asok, and further off
In the mistiness of Vidarbha.

At moments when life was too much a sea of sounds,
I had Banalata Sen of Natore and her wisdom
I remember her hair dark as night at Vidisha,
Her face an image of Sravasti as the pilot,
Undone in the blue milieu of the sea,
Never twice saw the earth of grass before him,
I have seen her, Banalata Sen of Natore.

When day is done, no fall somewhere but of dews
Dips into the dusk; the smell of the sun is gone
off the Kestrel's wings. Light is your wit now,
Fanning fireflies that pitch the wide things around.
For Banalata Sen of Natore.

For thousands of years, I have walked this earth,
From the seas of Ceylon to the waters of Malaya
I have traveled by night. I was there
in the grey worlds of Bimbisara and Asoka
and in the more distant dark, lost in the city of Vidarbha.
Lonely, tired, surrounded by the magic waves of life,
the only peace I found was with Banalata Sen of Natore.

Her face was like a sculpture from Shravasti;
as a helmless sailor lost in the far seas
watches green islands of spice rise before his eyes,
I saw her in that dark. Where have you been for so long?
asked Banalata Sen of Natore, raising her bird's nest eyes.

At day's end, dusk comes with the soft tread of dew
as the hawk wipes the smell of sunlight from its wings.
When all the colours of the earth fade,
the palimpsest prepares for tales in the twinkle of fireflies.
Birds wing homewards, rivers return.
All life's transactions cease. Only darkness remains
as I sit facing Banalata Sen.

I had Banalata Sen of Natore and her wisdom.

Jibanananda Das
(Translated by the poet)

Contributed By:

Pritish Nandy - A Padma Shri at 26, Pritish Nandy is a poet, designer, painter and photographer. He is credited with changing the face of Indian journalism and setting new standards of excellence at the now defunct *Illustrated Weekly of India*. After editing the *Observer of Business and Politics* and the *Sunday Observer*, he turned his attention to television where his interviews were feisty and provocative. Pritish Nandy Communications, a TV content boutique he founded, now produces several television programmes for national television. He is currently a member of the Rajya Sabha.

'This poem is special for me since it is the most magical love poem that I have ever read.'

My heart leaps up when I behold
  A rainbow in the sky:
So was it when my life began;
So is it now I am a man;
So be it when I shall grow old,
  Or let me die!
The Child is father of the Man;
  I could wish my days to be
Bound each to each by natural piety.

William Wordsworth

Contributed By:

Dr Jayant Narlikar - is a globally reputed scientist. Apart from his contribution to scientific research, Dr Narlikar has written books and articles in Marathi, Hindi and English at the non-technical level to popularize science. He has also written several science fiction stories and three novels in Marathi.

'This poem establishes an optimistic outlook and brings man close to nature.'

गायत्री मंत्र 80

ॐ भूर्भुवः स्वः
तत्सवितुर्वरेण्यम्
भर्गो देवस्य धीमहि
धियो यो नः प्रचोदयात

Gayatri Mantra

Oh God! Thou art the Giver of Life,
Remover of pain and sorrow,
The Bestower of happiness,
Oh! Creator of the Universe,
May we receive thy supreme sin-destroying light,
May Thou guide our intellect in the right direction.

Contributed By:

Nandan Nilekani - is the chief operating officer of Infosys. Together with Narayana Murthy, the CEO and co-founder of Infosys, he was recently named Businessmen of the Year' by *Fortune* magazine. In January 2006, he became one of the youngest entrepreneurs to join twenty global leaders on the prestigious World Economic Forum (WEF) foundation board. He is listed as one of the 100 most influential people in the world by *Time* magazine, 2006.

'The above lines of the Gayatri Mantra inspire you to live the best you can.'

Elegy Written in a Country Courtyard 81

The curfew tolls the knell of parting day,
The lowing herd wind slowly o'er the lea,
The ploughman homeward plods his weary way,
And leaves the world to darkness and to me.

Now fades the glimmering landscape on the sight,
And all the air a solemn stillness holds,
Save where the beetle wheels his droning flight,
And drowsy tinklings lull the distant folds;

Save that from yonder ivy-mantled tower
The moping owl does to the moon complain
Of such, as wandering near her secret bower,
Molest her ancient solitary reign.

Beneath those rugged elms, that yew-tree's shade,
Where heaves the turf in many a mouldering heap,
Each in his narrow cell for ever laid,
The rude forefathers of the hamlet sleep.

The breezy call of incense-breathing morn,
The swallow twittering from the straw-built shed,
The cock's shrill clarion, or the echoing horn,
No more shall rouse them from their lowly bed.

For them no more the blazing hearth shall burn,
Or busy housewife ply her evening care:
No children run to lisp their sire's return,
Or climb his knees the envied kiss to share.

Oft did the harvest to their sickle yield,
Their furrow oft the stubborn glebe has broke;
How jocund did they drive their team afield!
How bowed the woods beneath their sturdy stroke!

Let not Ambition mock their useful toil,
Their homely joys, and destiny obscure;
Nor Grandeur hear with a disdainful smile
The short and simple annals of the poor.

The boast of heraldry, the pomp of power,
And all that beauty, all that wealth e'er gave,
Awaits alike the inevitable hour—
The paths of glory lead but to the grave.

Nor you, ye Proud, impute to these the fault,
If Memory o'er their tomb no trophies raise,
Where through the long-drawn aisle and fretted vault
The pealing anthem swells the note of praise.

Can storied urn or animated bust
Back to its mansion call the fleeting breath?
Can Honour's voice provoke the silent dust,
Or Flattery soothe the dull cold ear of Death?

Perhaps in this neglected spot is laid
Some heart once pregnant with celestial fire;
Hands, that the rod of empire might have swayed
Or waked to ecstasy the living lyre.

But Knowledge to their eyes her ample page
Rich with the spoils of time, did ne'er unroll;
Chill Penury repressed their noble rage,
And froze the genial current of the soul.

Full many a gem of purest ray serene,
The dark unfathomed caves of ocean bear:
Full many a flower is born to blush unseen,
And waste its sweetness on the desert air.

Some village-Hampden, that with dauntless breast
The little tyrant of his fields withstood;
Some mute inglorious Milton here may rest,
Some Cromwell guiltless of his country's blood.

The applause of listening senates to command,
The threats of pain and ruin to despise,
To scatter plenty o'er a smiling land,
And read their history in a nation's eyes,

Their lot forbade: nor circumscribed alone
Their glowing virtues, but their crimes confined;
Forbade to wade through slaughter to a throne,
And shut the gates of mercy on mankind.

The struggling pangs of conscious truth to hide,
To quench the blushes of ingenuous shame,
Or heap the shrine of Luxury and Pride
With incense kindled at the Muse's flame.

Far from the madding crowd's ignoble strife,
Their sober wishes never leared to stray;
Along the cool sequester'd vale of life
They kept the noiseless tenor of their way.

Yet even these bones from insult to protect,
Some frail memorial still erected nigh.
With uncouth rhymes and shapeless sculpture decked,
Implores the passing tribute of a sigh.

Their name, their years, spelt by the unlettered muse,
The place of fame and elegy supply:
And many a holy text around she strews,
That teach the rustic moralist to die.

For who, to dumb Forgetfulness a prey,
This pleasing anxious being e'er resigned,
Left the warm precincts of the cheerful day,
Nor cast one longing, lingering look behind?

On some fond breast the parting soul relies,
Some pious drops the closing eye requires;
Ev'n from the tomb the voice of Nature cries,
Ev'n in our ashes live their wonted fires.

For thee, who mindful of the unhonoured dead
Dost in these lines their artless tale relate;
If chance, by lonely Contemplation led,
Some kindred spirit shall inquire thy fate.

Haply some hoary-headed swain may say,
'Oft have we seen him at the peep of dawn
Brushing with hasty steps the dews away
To meet the sun upon the upland lawn.

'There at the foot of yonder nodding beech
That wreathes its old fantastic roots so high,
His listless length at noontide would he stretch,
And pore upon the brook that babbles by.

'Hard by yon wood, now smiling as in scorn,
Mutt'ring his wayward fancies he would rove,
Now drooping, woeful-wan, like one forlorn,
Or crazed with care, or crossed in hopeless love.

'One morn I missed him on the customed hill,
Along the heath, and near his favourite tree;
Another came; nor yet beside the rill,
Nor up the lawn, nor at the wood was he;

'The next with dirges due in sad array
Slow through the church-way path we saw him borne.
Approach and read (for thou can'st read) the lay,
Grav'd on the stone beneath yon aged thorn.'

THE EPITAPH

Here rest his head upon the lap of Earth
A Youth to Fortune and to fame unknown.
Fair Science frowned not on his humble birth,
And Melancholy marked him for her own.

Large was his bounty, and his soul sincere,
Heaven did a recompense as largely send:
He gave to Misery all he had, a tear,
He gained from Heaven (t'was all he wished) a friend.

No farther seek his merits to disclose,
Or draw his frailties from their dread abode,
(There they alike in trembling hope repose),
The bosom of his Father and his God.

Thomas Gray

Contributed By:

Derek O'Brien - is India's premier quizmaster. He produces and hosts popular quiz shows on television and around the country. Derek loves a game of bridge, experimenting with exotic food, is passionate about horse racing and is the proud owner of a dozen fine horses.

'Well, for one it's a brilliant poem. However, what makes it special is this - my grandfather, a former Head of the Department of English of Banaras Hindu University and later Utkal University, explained the poem to me in detail, (in a truly memorable way), during a summer holiday I spent with him. I was in Class 9, but I will fondly treasure the experience that took place almost 25 years ago. I studied many poems thereafter in school and in college, but none better understood and appreciated than the one on that summer holiday 25 years ago!'

Khushwant Singh - is a renowned writer. The journalist and editor is also a historian, novelist, political commentator and social critic. He was a member of the Rajya Sabha and a diplomat in the ministry of external affairs. Memoirs, novels, joke books, books on religion, history, contemporary India and the women in his life - the range of his writing is diverse and fascinating.

'It is my favourite poem because it starts with a beautiful description of a rural scene at sunset. I proposed to a beautiful girl at the spot; she later became my wife.'

Quote 82

'Tis easy enough to be pleasant,
When life flows along like a song.
But the man worthwhile is the one who will smile,
When everything goes dead wrong.

Ella Wheeler Wilcox

Contributed By:

Piyush Pandey - is O&M India's executive chairman and national creative director. He has been inducted into Ogilvy's worldwide creative council, the global agency's famed inner circle that sets and evaluates creative standards. He has also been on the prestigious Cannes jury, and has won major awards for O&M's campaigns. He is an avid sports lover and was a tea taster before switching to advertising.

'From memories of childhood, it's been my guiding principle.'

The Treasured Writings of Khalil Gibran: The Playground of Life **83**

One hour devoted to the pursuit of Beauty
And Love is worth a full century of glory
Given by the frightened weak to the strong.
From that hour comes man's Truth; and
During that century Truth sleeps between
The restless arms of disturbing dreams.

In that hour the soul sees for herself
The Natural Law, and for that century she
Imprisons herself behind the law of man;
And she is shackled with irons of oppression.

In that hour was the inspiration of the Songs
Of Solomon, and that century was the blind
Power which destroyed the temple of Baalbek.

That hour was the birth of the Sermon on the
Mount, and that century wrecked the castles of
Palmyra and the tower of Babylon.

That hour was the Hegira of Mohammed, and that
Century forgot Allah, Golgotha, and Sinai.
One hour devoted to the mourning and lamenting the
Stolen equality of the weak is nobler than a
Century filled with greed and usurpation.

It is at that hour when the heart is
Purified by flaming sorrow, and
Illuminated by the torch of Love.

And in that century, desires for Truth
Are buried in the bosom of the earth.

That hour is the root which must flourish.
That hour is the hour of contemplation,
The hour of meditation, the hour of
Prayer, and the hour of a new era of good.

And that century is a life of Nero spent
On self-investment taken solely from
Earthly substance.

This is life.
Portrayed on the stage for ages;
Recorded earthily for centuries;
Lived in strangeness for years;
Sung as a hymn for days;
Exalted for but an hour, but the
Hour is treasured by Eternity as a jewel.

Khalil Gibran

Contributed By:

Deepak Parekh - As the chairman of HDFC, Infrastructure Development Corporation and many other companies, Deepak Parekh is one of India's most prominent and socially conscious business executives.

The Heart of the Tree 84

What does he plant who plants a tree?
He plants a friend of sun and sky;
He plants the flag of breezes free;
The shaft of beauty, towering high.
He plants a home to heaven anigh
For song and mother-croon of bird
In hushed and happy twilight heard —
The treble of heaven's harmony —
These things he plants who plants a tree.

What does he plant who plants a tree?
He plants cool shade and tender rain,
And seed and bud of days to be,
And years that fade and flush again;
He plants the glory of the plain;
He plants the forest's heritage;
The harvest of a coming age;
The joy that unborn eyes shall see —
These things he plants who plants a tree.

What does he plant who plants a tree?
He plants, in sap and leaf and wood,
In love of home and loyalty
And far-cast thought of civic good —
His blessing in the neighbourhood
Who in the hollow of His hand
Holds all the growth of all our land —

A nation's growth from sea to sea
Stirs in his heart who plants a tree.

Henry Ceyler Bunner

Contributed By:

I. G. Patel - is an economist and the former governor of the Reserve Bank of India. He has also been the director of IIM, Ahmedabad and the London School of Economics. He now lives in Baroda.

'It beautifully conveys the importance of protecting the environment.'

Brahma 85

If the red slayer think he slays,
Or if the slain think he is slain,
They know not well the subtle ways
I keep, and pass, and turn again.

Far or forgot to me is near;
Shadow and sunlight are the same;
The vanished gods to me appear;
And one to me are shame and fame.

They reckon ill who leave me out;
When me they fly, I am the wings;
I am the doubter and the doubt,
And I the hymn the Brahmin sings.

The strong gods pine for my abode,
And pine in vain the sacred Seven;
But thou, meek lover of the good!
Find me, and turn thy back on heaven.

Ralph Waldo Emerson

Contributed By:

Justice R. S. Pathak - The former chief justice of India and judge of the International Court at the Hague has many publications in reputed law journals. Once an eminent jurist of the Himachal Pradesh High Court, he is a member of the executive body of Indian Council for Social Welfare, the Bharatiya Sanskriti Parishad and other corporate bodies.

'It teaches us that God is everywhere, that he is present in every species of life and in all forms of existence, and that those who lead a good life will find God in this life itself without having to wait to go to Heaven for that purpose.'

On the Banks of the Indrayani 86

On the banks of the Indrayani,
In God's Aalandi,
Is the samadhi of Dnyaneshwar.
The Vaishnavas dance to and fro,
Gaining inspiration from Wisdom's King
Back and forth, but at the heart is that sacred tree, the enlightened soul
Enlightened they remain, having been enlightened,
Nivrati, Sopaan, Muktabai.

G.D. Madgulkar

Contributed By:

Pandit Bhimsen Joshi - has been a musical adventurer for most of his life. Pre-eminent in the Kirana gharana, he excels in *gamakar*, *meend* and *tanakriya*. Through amalgamating various *gayaki* styles, and his own introspective reflections, he has created an incomparable blend and repertoire. His seeming effortlessness is the result of relentless *riyaz*: his listeners say his soothing ragas appear to surround and wrap themselves around you from all sides. This renaissance musician is a Padma Shri, Padma Bhushan and Sangeet Natak Akademi awardee.

Copyright Acknowledgements

Grateful acknowledgement is made to the following for permission to reprint copyright material:

Faber and Faber Ltd for 'Epitaph for a Tyrant' in *Collected Shorter Poems* by W. H. Auden, and for 'The City' by C.P. Cavafy translated by Lawrence Durrell in *The Alexandria Quartet* by Lawrence Durrell

Henry Holt and Company for 'The Road Not Taken' by Robert Frost

Dover Publications for 'Stopping by Woods on a Snowy Evening' by Robert Frost

Tharpa Publications for *Guide to the Bodhisattva's Way of Life*

Virago Press, a division of Time Warner Book Group UK for 'And I Still Rise', reproduced from *The Complete Collected Poems* by Maya Angelou

The Little Magzine: Looking for Me, Vol. IV, Issue 5&6, Delhi, 2003, Website *www.littlemag.com*.

